A *Shaker* Musical Legacy

MW00379066

Frontispiece. Brother Ricardo Belden, last male Shaker at Hancock, Massachusetts. AUTHORS' COLLECTION.

A *Shaker* Musical Legacy

Robert C. Opdahl and Viola E. Woodruff Opdahl

University Press of New England

Hanover and London

Published by University Press of New England

One Court Street, Lebanon, NH 03766

www.upne.com

© 2004 by University Press of New England

Printed in the United States of America

5 4 3 2 1

All rights reserved. No part of this book may be reproduced in any form or by any electronic or mechanical means, including storage and retrieval systems, without permission in writing from the publisher, except by a reviewer, who may quote brief passages in a review. Members of educational institutions and organizations wishing to photocopy any of the work for classroom use, or authors and publishers who would like to obtain permission for any of the material in the work, should contact Permissions, University Press of New England, One Court Street, Lebanon, NH 03766.

ISBN: 1–58465–360–4

LC: 2004101639

~

To the memory of Jerome and Sybil Count, whose

deep respect for the Shakers and close friendship

with Brother Ricardo Belden set in motion a series

of events that made this book possible.

O thou, my soul, arise and sing

Let grateful paeans loudly ring

Let holy raptures praise thy King

   —Song 95; O thou, my soul, arise and sing

Contents

Illustrations

Foreword

This book arose from a chain of unlikely events in which I was an unwitting link. It reaches back from the present time to over one hundred fifty years ago, when the United Society, at its peak, was singing and dancing before God in ordered ranks, yet at certain times, freely and ecstatically as individuals—a time when the Shakers were in prime vigor and strength, steadfast in their traditions.

Random happenstance, blind circumstance, and dumb luck formed the fragile links of the wiggly chain upon which this unique book depends. I say "unique" confidently, for it contains much material not in any other publication. It allows direct comparisons—on facing pages—of the simplicity of the original Shaker song format with the authors' editing into standard notation for modern use. It speaks to scholars, to choral songsters, to lovers of music first meeting the Shakers on its pages. It speaks also to those who would know in detail how the Shakers worshiped God with their "entire bodies."

On an early summer Thursday in 1948, Margot Mayo—folklorist, mentor, friend, and leader of our folklore recording expedition to Appalachia for the Library of Congress in 1946—called. Was I free for the weekend? College had freed me for the summer; I only waited lazily for the next Monday, when I would drive up to the Adirondacks for the "Grand Opening" of a new resort in which I'd be the featured entertainer. Without quite understanding what I was in for, I found myself hastily packed, driving up past lovely scenes of the Hudson River, taking Margot to the Shaker Village Work Camp in New Lebanon, New York.

En route Margot told me of the Shakers' history, doctrines, customs, and music and dance worship services. Raised by two generations of Pentecostal Missionaries, I was not very surprised by the idea of dancing during worship—I was raised hearing "tongues" and mass glossolalia in Chinese and English syllables, and witnessing individual ecstatic movements.

She also told me about the camp. Jerry and Sybil Count, a couple from New York City, were deeply concerned about the frequent lack of self-confidence among children of the upper middle class. They felt this was caused by living under the care of a succession of servants, being sent off for most of their lives to boarding schools, and being exiled each summer to trivial, non-challenging activities in the typical camps of that time. Having met with no personal challenges and no personal responsibilities, these teenaged children had gained no triumphs, had achieved no successes to look back on. They were generally not badly spoiled children, Margot pointed out—who was there to spoil them?

Jerry and Sybil conceived the idea of a summer camp in which the children would work on significant projects, in significant workshops, and would be challenged to meet high standards of performance. As in a college, they would have to register for workshops (but every two weeks, not every semester) dividing their limited time according to their own priorities and to the workshop space available. Hard choices for those who had never made a significant choice before. Workshops would consist of photography, care of the camp's horses, modern dance, raising poultry, wood shop, gardening, cooking for the camp once a week, pottery, graphic arts, and so on. Everyone also took part in "all-camp activities" such as blueberry harvesting on top of Mount Lebanon or choral singing of Bach and Handel oratorios and other challenging music. No distinction was made between the arts and the manual work; campers would have to take on both.

As plans developed, the Counts started looking for sites. By accident, they came across the New Lebanon South Family, whose extensive buildings and grounds were being evacuated and sold by the remaining Shakers, who were moving to the nearby Hancock, Massachusetts, Shaker colony. The Counts learned about the Shakers' high standards of conduct and workmanship, their forsaking of material ownership and pride, their fabled tolerance, gender equality, and non-violence. The Shakers learned of the Counts' plans and ideals for a youth camp and heartily approved sale for that use. The Shaker Village Work Camp opened in 1947 not only with Shaker approval but also with frequent appearances of those Shakers who could still get around.

I spent that weekend at the camp as Margot's guest but couldn't resist getting involved. Being an engineering student, I helped plan the lifting of the huge old Shaker chair factory for necessary repairs to its foundation. I helped the staff here and there. I called a square dance, got out my banjo, and sang folk songs to all that Saturday evening.

Sunday noon Jerry Count asked me into his office. The campers had just held a town meeting. After voting to change their bedtime hour, they voted to instruct Jerry to hire me. Jerry explained that the camp had no money to pay me, but if I stayed on I would be fed and housed. I was touched, of course, but explained that I had to leave to appear for my contracted (and renewable) engagement at the new lodge in the Adirondacks. Later I drove quietly away, trying not to be noticed, feeling a bit like a soldier going AWOL.

The Lodge, as I'll call it, was lovely and lively. I had "dream duty"—only an hour's official entertainment each day, usually square dance instruction or folk singing. There could be no happier or better job for a young, single, male combat veteran, could there? Somewhat surprised, I found myself driving back to New Lebanon after refusing the Lodge manager's enthusiastic offer of renewal for the summer.

At the start of that camp season, the home economics person had failed to show up. The Counts rushed down the mountain to the town of New Lebanon to track down the high school home economics teacher—the statuesque, beautiful, ever-sunny Gloria Eldredge Wagner. She agreed to take over home arts workshops at the camp. On the day decreed for duck slaughter, Gloria found herself alone; the workshop members had all deserted. I volunteered to help. With farm experience and bloody combat behind me, I coolly killed the two dozen ducks, but plucking them was something else. No one had known to bring wax for that chore. So the two of us sat a-plucking with pained thumbs for hours, and I found myself reciting the story of my recent disengagement from a very painful love affair. To skip ahead a year, Gloria's and my wedding on the ninth of July, 1949, was an "all-camp activity" at the nearby Episcopal Church.

Despite the Shakers' espousal of celibacy and rejection of marriage, Fannie Estabrook, the Eldress at Hancock, attended our wedding. She was the person of highest spiritual rank at Hancock colony—Elders and Eldresses were responsible for spiritual wellbeing, while Deacons and Deaconesses administered secular affairs within the community.

The best man at our wedding was my college housemate,

college squaredance band pianist, and best buddy, Bob Opdahl. The bridesmaid was tiny, bright Viola Woodruff, Gloria's fellow teacher and best friend at New Lebanon High School. Bob and Viola had been introduced to each other by matchmaker Gloria, an introduction that took as a "slow fire" and luckily not a "hang fire." I got them both deeply interested in banjo, folk, and Shaker music. In fact, during spring break in 1949, the four of us went on a successful folk music recording trip to Tennessee.

A frequent visitor to my work in the wood shop and on the repair of the chair factory at Shaker Village was Brother Ricardo Belden. He was the last male Shaker in the entire area, and the linchpin of this book. He had been taken in by the Shakers at Enfield, Connecticut, prior to age ten, some seventy-odd years before. He had been taught and cared for by Shakers, who had been in their prime during the Civil War days. He had sung and danced in worship services when those were regular events, and when spectators still took trains from New York City to gawk at the peculiar worship "antics" of this strange sect.

Brother Ricardo was a prime woodcraft man: once a maker of fine wooden clocks, his later life was devoted to the repair and rebuilding of wooden clocks owned by museums. He was an extremely valuable asset to me in both the woodworking shop and in chair factory repair. I can close my eyes and see him vividly—feet spread apart a bit, hands behind him with thumbs clasped to each other, right palm outward in front of the left, wearing plain, unpressed trousers and a clean unpressed shirt—watching silently until he saw a need to speak up, in his dry, thin old Yankee speech, or recite a warning, or suggestion, quietly into my ear. His skin was pale and his eyes bright blue, setting off his marvelously white hair and neatly trimmed, white, round-the-jaw beard. Though short of stature and slight of build, he dominated the room without effort or intent.

In one workshop, the campers made homemade banjos out of large wooden salad bowls. As with all the other activities at the camp, Brother Ricardo was interested especially in workmanship. Despite the early, long-lasting Shaker disdain of musical instruments, he praised and encouraged the banjo-making campers. When he found out I was planning to make a copy of a homemade octagonal box banjo I had photographed and recorded in Kentucky, he brought me a large piece of aged black walnut from his precious stock. Over the next two years he instructed me in the finer techniques of hand tools, such as the scary unguarded-blade drawknife, and gently pushed me into making the banjo almost entirely by hand. It is still a fine-sounding, pretty instrument.

At camp's end each season, the staff and campers put on

workshop demonstrations for parents and visitors. Photos, drawings, paintings, and carvings were displayed; square dances, modern dances, and choral works were performed. Most spectators were astonished at the levels attained by the campers. In 1950 someone suggested that we put on a replica of a Shaker dance worship service. Enthusiasm was universal among the staff, so Brother Ricardo was approached for permission from the Eldress. Permission came with the proviso that the service be performed reverently, with the participants acting in the stead of those Shakers who could no longer dance, and for their sakes. Brother Ricardo, still being able, would teach us and participate. He left a hymn book from which we were to learn "Life, Life, Living Zeal." He would return to start rehearsals in a couple of days. When this news was announced by the staff, the campers were unanimously excited, and they promised to learn and perform by the rules laid down by the Shakers.

When the day arrived for the first rehearsal, the music and dance staff gathered at the piano before lunch to run through the chosen first song. Margot, Hal Aks, who was the choral director and baseball coach, and I were dismayed to find a system of musical notation we could not read. Had it been the English tonic sol fa system, Hal could have read it with a little difficulty. Like tonic sol fa, this notation used letters of the alphabet, but damned few; the rest were symbols meaningless to us. Lunch forgotten, and Brother Ricardo's visit fast approaching, we madly guessed and tried, again and again. Finally I took a pad and began treating the tune like a code, looking for repeating patterns in the Shaker notation. I chose a pattern near the end of the song, since Margot insisted the last note of the song should be "do." Hal guessed at the notes in the pattern preceding the "do" and, using standard notation, transcribed the entire song. It worked! In a few minutes we could sing "Life, Life, Living Zeal," taking rhythmic clues from the words. (See page 188.) Brother Ricardo arrived, corrected our rhythms, and we joined the campers for our first learning session. He was an excellent teacher; in an hour the entire camp could sing and dance our first Shaker selection. What Brother Ricardo no longer could do physically, he described so graphically and economically that we had few problems comprehending it.

As we learned more dances and songs in the next few weeks, our enthusiasm soared. Margot and I, ever concerned with folk techniques, held a private session with Brother Ricardo. We verified that he sang in the self-decorated, archaic "vocal" manner, ornamented with the subtle "slides," "scoops," and "warbles" used by oldtime Appalachian a cappella ballad singers—in classical music, these ornaments were known as "appoggiatura" and "trills." Yet he pointed out that the Shakers were theoretically strongly opposed to "deco-

rated music." This term included prolonged trills (à la Handel, et al.) and the holding of long notes at the ends of phrases to their full values. Harmony was strictly forbidden. We gathered that Shaker women did not sharply "turn" their phrase-ending notes upward, either. Brother Ricardo seemed totally unconscious of the subtle decorations in his own singing, for these were actually the minimized stylistic touches of the "musically untrained"—not classically trained, that is—general population from which he came and with whom he lived for much of his life. Aside from the extra effort that precise notation would have required, and its being more difficult for the general population to read, the Shaker notation transcribers, like many classical composers, rarely noted down these subtle decorations, instead taking them for granted. To my knowledge, only occasionally did even a "grace note" appear in a Shaker song manuscript. Embellishments added to "Simple Gifts" in section ten of this book illustrate the subtleties we heard in Brother Ricardo's voice as he sang the song. Margot and I decided that to teach everyone this style would be too time-consuming, and we agreed to strive merely for clarity, unity, and shortened final notes. Even so, several natural mimics picked up the subtleties just from hearing Brother Ricardo's (and our) examples.

The dance service was presented during parents' weekend. Eldress Fanny Estabrook and some of the Hancock Sisters came with Brother Ricardo to the camp and sat primly near the dance floor. Brother Ricardo appeared in front of the audience as a Deacon and sternly lectured the "World's People" on behavior, as his predecessor Deacons had done generations before: the World's People were not to applaud, they were to be respectful of this worship—no matter how peculiar it might seem—and the young dancers were dancing for all Shakers who could not themselves dance. "The World's People," he continued, "worship God with their voices, we Believers worship Him with our voices, and our whole bodies; like David before the Ark . . . The Worlds' People may breed, but we Believers may not; we forsake earthly love; we dedicate our entire lives and energy to God." Gentle, oak-ribbed Ricardo Belden held all in awed silence as the substitute Shakers marched silently in.

Despite being teenaged children, the campers projected dignity and piety, joy and holy ecstasy, as they sang and danced through the service. There was total silence from the audience as they "worshiped" in the Shaker's stead, then filed out of sight. A long, long pause, and then tumultuous applause arose, sustained madly for minutes. One easily found tears in astonished parents' eyes, in the Shakers' grateful eyes, in proud staff members' eyes.

About three months before our wedding, we had introduced Bob and Viola to the Shaker Village Work Camp and to Jerry and Sybil Count. The Counts immediately hired both Bob and Viola for early summer temporary jobs at Shaker Village. It was a long enough stint to thoroughly convince both Bob and Viola to return the next summer as full-time staff.

Gloria's and my last summer (1950) at Shaker Village coincided with Bob and Viola's first full summer there. Bob and I, and another staff member, Johnny O'Leary—like me, one of Margot's "kids"—worked closely with the campers in the folk music and dance workshops, the woodshop, on rebuilding projects, and in Shaker music and dance workshops. Bob and Viola fit right into camp life and became increasingly interested in Shaker lore. It didn't take long for Brother Ricardo to became Bob's close friend and advisor. I learned later that Bob continued as a staff member in those same workshops for the next five summers. In some seasons he worked closely with Johnny O'Leary, a fine caller; Bob is himself a fine squaredance pianist. Bob was later joined by a new staff member, Bert Sonnenfeld. Bert had started as a shy camper during my first year. Viola became deeply involved in Shaker cookery, music research, and clothing design. In between transcribing Shaker songs, she supervised making the Shaker outfits for the annual presentations of Shaker music and dance at the ends of camp sessions.

One day Viola and Bob married, much to Gloria's smug satisfaction. Bob went into mathematics, and later computers. Gloria and I moved to the Southwest and inadvertently lost touch with the Opdahls. Nineteen years passed. Eventually I wrote the Opdahls at an address I had at last located. It was wrong! However, an accommodating and kind postmaster rerouted it to the right town not far from him—nearby Hurley, New York. We soon after reunited with the Opdahls.

Brother Ricardo had given Jerry Count nine Shaker song books over the years; Jerry allowed Bob access to all nine. Bob mastered all of the five different notation systems in them and could sightread from them all. Jerry died in 1968; two years later Sybil, unreservedly, gave all nine Shaker music manuscript books to the Opdahls with a look in her eyes that said, "See here, 'Bopdahl,' get as many of these songs as possible off the pages and into the light of day!"

Gloria and I got very excited when they told us that they were seriously thinking of publishing, and we heartily and continuously encouraged—and nagged—them to do so. I have delighted in seeing the work progress and feel greatly privileged to be asked to contribute to it. One of our most valuable contributions was the introduction to the Opdahls of historical musicologist Dr. Joanna Ching-yun Lee, who had been our guide, translator, and amanuensis during two

folksong concert tours of China, Hong Kong, and Tibet. Before she could catch her breath, she found herself enthralled with the project.

At the same time, Bob and Viola invited Barbara B. Zimet, of nearby Woodstock, to be a musical consultant on the book project. Barbara, a well-known pianist, piano teacher, and consultant, was unable to accept the invitation for two years. Then Joanna and Barbara worked as co-consultants until Joanna had to honor other commitments, such as teaching at the University of Hong Kong for an extended period of time. Barbara than proceeded as the sole music consultant.

Today, Shaker music is appreciated solely as a musical art expression. Often it is treated as raw material suitable chiefly for refinement. Its dance function is frequently forgotten, unknown, or ignored. Recordings are issued, with Shaker songs rendered almost sterile by highly cultured, formally trained voices. These voices produced highly rounded, Italianate vowels through open throats and rounded, open mouths, with chest tones predominating. The Shakers, and the general population at their time, pronounced vowels as in speech, singing through tense throats, with head tones predominating.

Singers and instrumentalists linger languidly over "Simple Gifts," not realizing the speed and vigor necessary to accompany the Square Order Shuffle, a Shaker dance described in the last section of this book. Compare these arrangements with the modern song "Lord of the Dance," which is set to an adaptation of the music of "Simple Gifts," In the versions I have heard, it is set to the proper speed and performed in the proper spirit. Many Shaker compositions were composed or arranged to be dance music, to be "labored" to, marched to, gestured to, with strict dance rhythm and often with vigor. The music in this unusual book (and all Shaker collections) should be sung—better yet, sung and danced to, if it was intended as a dance tune—with the underlying dance in mind "in the stead of the Shakers." Four full dances are provided herein for those choral groups that might wish to bring a more profound Shaker image to their audiences.

This book is a work of loving labor by the dedicated authors, and it was years in the making. It is a tribute to the United Society of the Believers in Christ's Second Coming—particularly to Brother Ricardo Belden—by all who contributed to this volume, including those who came to know him only through this work. We, all of us involved, gratefully consider the material in *Rise and Sing* to be a "spirit gift" to the "Sons of Adam" from Mother Ann and her followers—as delivered by the ever-capable Brother Ricardo.

STU JAMIESON

Preface

Background

Devotees of Shaker history are well aware that a small group of Shakers, including founder Mother Ann Lee, emigrated from England to New York State in 1774. By the latter part of the nineteenth century, rapid social and economic changes in America contributed to a decline in the number of converts. A society that once numbered in the four figures now has fewer than one dozen members residing at New Gloucester (Sabbathday Lake), Maine, the last active Shaker community.

The Shaker impact on architecture, furniture style, invention, and the American work ethic is impressive; however, it is their music that is the special provenance of this book. Long before beginning serious work on it, we had read Edward D. Andrew's book, *The Gift to Be Simple.*[1] We felt particularly drawn to his commentaries on some of the same songs that Brother Ricardo Belden had known from boyhood and sung for us at Shaker Village. In 1989, Bess Hawes, at the time director of the Folk Arts Program of the National Endowment for the Arts, referred us to Daniel Patterson's *The Shaker Spiritual.*[2] In 1960, Patterson had journeyed to existing Shaker communities, Shaker museums, and known sites of private collectors to locate as many existing song manuscripts as possible. He found over eight hundred. His success was notable in that only about fifty-five additional manuscripts had surfaced by the end of the century.[3] This search also provided him with a vast number of songs, and with information on scribes, musicians, music notation, singing style, the folk nature of Shaker music, and Shaker history, as well as the opportunity to talk with Shakers still living at the time.

Whenever we spent research time at the Shaker Library and Museum in Old Chatham, New York, Jerry Grant, the director of research at the site, cheered us on and directed us to relevant Shaker journals, letters, drawings, photographs, and music theory books. One of the significant sources that

he brought to our attention was Harold Cook's *Shaker Music,* a doctoral dissertation that was published posthumously in 1973.[4] This source, along with Andrew's *Gift to Be Simple* and Patterson's *The Shaker Spiritual,* contains an enormous amount of the groundwork necessary to anyone working on Shaker song manuscripts.

Twenty years after the publication of Cook's *Shaker Music,* Stephen Stein's impressive book, *The Shaker Experience in America,* appeared. Stein's description of the New Lebanon Shakers' enjoyment of their festive outings at nearby Queechy Lake in Canaan, New York, awakened memories for us.[5] His account took us back to the late 1940s, when "Uncle Bill," a lifelong Lebanon Springs resident, entertained us with reminiscences of hiring out to work for the Shakers in his younger days. One of his often repeated recollections was of the joyous times the Lebanon Shakers had experienced within his lifetime, picnicking, boating, singing, and holding worship services at Queechy Lake.

In 1970, Sybil Count gave us a fantastic gift—a collection of nine Shaker song manuscripts! At the time she confirmed that Brother Ricardo Belden, the last male at the Hancock Shaker community, had given them to her late husband, Jerry, during the late 1940s and early 1950s. No other gift could have better expressed Brother Ricardo's appreciation for Jerry's quiet but transparent respect for and interest in preserving the Shaker songs.

So why did Sybil give them to us? A meaningful answer to this question requires some background information. The story of our interest in the Shakers and their music begins a little more than fifty years ago, when we first met at what was then called the Shaker Village Work Camp, situated on what had been the South Family site of the New Lebanon Shaker community. We knew, by way of the local grapevine, that the Counts had purchased the property in 1947 for use as a summer work experience for adolescents. The staff and villagers familiarly referred to the site as "Shaker Village," as we do in this book, but its official title was, at first, "Shaker Village Work Camp," later changed to "Shaker Village Work Group" and still later to "Work Education Foundation, Inc." The purchase represented a fulfillment of the Counts' dream to provide a summer experience work project for teenagers who had never or had seldom worked with their hands. When the Counts realized the nature of the property they had acquired, they began to take on the mantle of a second stewardship—one that involved the preservation of and appreciation for the Shaker heritage of the site.

By 1948, Shaker Village had became a fully functioning reality. The workshop program, mentioned in the foreword, included workshops on Shaker music, dance, industry, and the routine of everyday life. The villagers restored the chair shop, reproduced Shaker boxes, respectfully reenacted Shaker dances, made Shaker outfits for these reenactments, learned Shaker songs, and collected and used Shaker recipes. In the process, they learned about Shaker beliefs, work ethics, and craftsmanship.

Jerry Count came up with his plans, organized them, and made them reality. His knowledge was extensive and his enthusiasm contagious. Sybil Count had a very natural ability to mediate person-to-person relationships on a daily basis. Together, they made their dream work. In doing so, they earned the respect and gratitude of the Shakers still residing at Hancock. Their dedication to helping adolescents and to protecting Shaker heritage made a strong impression on us. We also felt privileged to have the opportunity to meet the Shakers still residing at Hancock and to have access to the Shaker music manuscripts.

Before our appearance at Shaker Village, staff members from New York—Robert Stuart Jamieson (Stu), folk musician and writer; Margot Mayo, founder of the American Square Dance Group; and Hal Aks, director of the Interracial Fellowship Chorus—had already begun to transcribe a few Shaker songs. They were eager to use Shaker songs in the performance programs presented each season at Shaker Village. When we became fulltime staff members two seasons later in 1950, we became active in the many Shaker-oriented workshops.

Of lasting significance to us during the several summers we served on the staff was the opportunity to participate in the ongoing project of transcribing and testing songs used for workshops and performances. The onsite availability of the manuscripts and the frequent consultations with Brother Ricardo Belden at Hancock made the project very inviting. This undertaking was further fueled by staff members Bert Sonnenfeld and John O'Leary, who contributed their special talents to help bring the songs and dances back to life. This workshop experience led to recordings, on sale to the pub-

lic, and to public performances in what had once been the South family chair factory. The work on Shaker music attracted the attention of a regional publication and led to a feature story on how staff members and villagers at Shaker Village were immersed in the research, transcription, and performance of Shaker songs and dances.[6]

The music staff members savored the opportunity to consult with Brother Ricardo Belden, who had been a Shaker for most of his life. In an interview in 1952 in which Jerry Count asked him how long he had been a member, Brother Ricardo replied, "I was brought to Enfield, Connecticut [i.e., a Shaker community], on July 30, 1874, when I was four years old."[7] He clarified the meaning of membership in response to a later question: "We are members of a Shaker Community at twenty-one years old, when we are old enough to sign the covenant that all are asked to sign when they reach the age of twenty-one."[8]

Especially valuable for the music workshops were Brother Ricardo's firsthand accounts about *how* the Shakers, throughout his past, sang the songs, when they sang them, and how they performed the dances. He volunteered information about tempo, vocable syllables, dance patterns, and appropriate occasions for using the different songs. It was a privilege to observe Brother Ricardo, in modest attire, giving careful attention to any questions asked of him but subtly keeping his distance from female staff members and teenagers. Sybil Count once described him as a "very active, intelligent man with a wide range of interests."[9]

Now back to the question "Why give those manuscripts to us?" We were actively involved at Shaker Village during 1950–55. Even when our onsite involvement ended, we continued to work on the Shaker music project as time permitted. After Jerry's death in 1968, Sybil kept Shaker Village open for another season, and then, because she found the task too overwhelming for one person, she closed the project and sold the site. Even after the closing and the sale, we maintained our contacts with Sybil. In 1970, she gave the nine manuscripts to us with the hope that the song transcription project would continue to move ahead.

During the early 1990s we began to devote large blocks of time to this project. We kept Sybil well abreast of our progress by phone and visits until her death in 1996. In a sense, our approach to transcribing and editing selected Shaker songs is a narrow one, since we have limited our efforts to just nine manuscripts out of the 855 known to be extant. Fortunately, these nine offer a variety of song types, notations, time periods, and content. They serve as symbols of pleasant memories of the Counts and Brother Ricardo while providing an opportunity to fulfill their dreams of making more Shaker songs available for actual use.

The Shaker Songs

We have selected 122 songs out of the over nine hundred contained in the nine manuscripts. This book also includes four songs—"I'm on my way to Zion," "Ine Vine Violet," "Love, O, Love," and "Precept on Precept"—that we have been unable to find in any of the nine manuscripts. We learned them directly from Brother Ricardo, who also taught the Shaker dance steps and motions that he paired with "Precept on Precept," "Who will bow and bend like a willow," "Life, Life Living Zeal," and "Simple Gifts." Discerning readers will note that the last three, with minor differences, appear elsewhere in this book, since they are among the songs appearing in the manuscripts. Stu Jamieson has a clear memory of Brother Ricardo saying that the Shakers sang these songs "with vigor, celerity, and an outpouring of gladness and joy."[10]

An ID code appears in the upper lefthand corner of each song page and includes the letters we have assigned to identify the manuscript as well as the page number of the song in the original manuscript. It also includes, in boldface, Daniel Patterson's checklist numbers for the manuscripts in our collection that he had examined at the time he was gathering data for his book *The Shaker Spiritual*. For example, the complete identification code for "A Laughing Song" in Manuscript A is "MS SV-A/**SU-2**, pp. 225–226." "SV" stands for "Shaker Village Work Camp," where Jerry Count received the manuscripts from Brother Ricardo Belden. The "A" identifies the first and oldest manuscript in our collection. "**SU-2**" is Patterson's checklist number.

During the 1820s and 1840s two Shakers, Russel Haskell and Isaac Youngs, both of whom were knowledgeable about musical form, expressed concern about what they felt was a general musical illiteracy and a lack of uniformity in the Shaker communities that they visited. Haskell wrote to Youngs, "I wish you success in your laudable undertaking to improve the system of musical instruction, and produce a uniformity in the matter of writing music."[11]

It is not easy to sort out the varied meter and tempo instructions provided by the Shaker musicians, particularly for the earlier Shaker songs. There often was a lack of agreement among them and, even more often, a lack of understanding or compliance by the general population of Shakers. Musicians like Haskell, Youngs, and Harvey L. Eades worked out modes of time, signatures, and metronome readings in table format for the edification of the Shakers. Youngs was also among those who constructed devices to aid the Shakers in determining the tempo of any given song. His "mode-ometer" consisted of a pendulum with a sliding device that could be positioned at any given point on a coded scale to indicate the tempo of a song.

Neither such devices as this nor instruction books by the learned Shaker musicians instilled the hoped-for level of uniformity. On 16 October 1841, Andrew Houston of Union Village, Ohio, wrote a letter in "diffidence and reluctance" to Isaac Youngs in which he courteously but firmly challenged Youngs's proposals to improve, refine, and make consistent the Shaker modes.

> We find no serious difficulty whatever, in communicating any kind of a song, from place to place in this country, when noted anything like correct according to the Rules: and what more do we want than this? The fewer the details or ramifications any science can be made to have the better, . . . We do not feel able to reconcile ourselves as yet, to the idea of adopting 16 or 18 moods. Simply, good brother, because we humbly, and I trust honestly, believe it altogether unnecessary for any practical or useful purposes whatever. . . . I think we should not find one person in fifty, that have minds of a construction, calculated to describe among such subtleties & nice distinctions as our good Brother Isaac. . . . How can it be expected that we shall all sing a given tune the same speed when we attempt to test it by this ordeal?[12]

Entering songs into manuscript books did not guarantee that the Shakers in the various communities would sing any given song in the same manner. They were more likely to sing songs as their spirit, the immediate occasion, or their community traditions moved them, just as ethnic and religious groups around the world have tended to do. This was especially true when tempo, timing, bars, and notes were missing in the manuscripts. These missing notations provide a picturesqueness in the transcript versions of the songs that is lacking in our "updated" edited versions.

Echoes of this kind of individuality may be found in the writings of John and Alan Lomax, who, almost a century later, protested against the standardization of folk music: "Worse than thieves are ballad collectors, for when they capture and imprison in cold type a folk song, at the same time they kill it. Its change and growth are not so likely to continue after a fixed model for comparison exists."[13]

Charles and Ruth Seeger, in the musical foreword they wrote for John and Alan Lomax's 1947 collection *Best Loved American Folk Songs*, also expressed concern about reducing a folk song to one single denominator. On the second page of their foreword, they discoursed on the difficulty of assigning folk songs to print: "Perhaps one of the most extensive departures from folk idiom . . . is the employment of a single written tune and setting for all stanzas of a song. Folk singers customarily vary the tune. . . . The subtle variation given by a particular singer possesses an artistic quality lost in the printed single melody and its arrangement."[14]

Discussions at Shaker Village about the use of vocables, syllables without English meaning that were used in wordless songs, centered on the possibility of a variant pronunciation of "lo" as being "loo" or "lu." Today, some listeners who were at Shaker Village when Brother Ricardo visited there argue that he sang the variant "loo, loo"; others insist that he sang "lo, lo." We have not seen, in any unpublished manuscripts or in any published materials by the Shakers, the use of "loo loo loo" vocables except in an anonymous letter written in May 1801 to Thomas Brown, a man who had once been a Shaker. The writer of the letter criticized the Shakers for their use of vocables rather than recognizable words of praise in their songs. Brown's unhappy correspondent wrote "We do not so much as hear of tunes in the songs of Moses, or Deborah, or any of the rejoicing saints, before David's time. He seems to have been the first that instituted tunes. . . . It appears . . . singing did not consist in singing loo loo loo. . . . In all the scriptures, we hear nothing of singing tunes without words."[15]

There is common agreement that Brother Ricardo used only a single syllable vocable such as "lo" for all of the songs, or parts thereof, that required vocables. He distinguished between quarter-note vocables and eighth-note vocables, for example, by allotting to a "lo" on a quarter note twice the time value that he gave to a "lo" on an eighth note.

Our introduction to the Shaker use of a folk/ballad type of embellishment occurred when we heard Brother Ricardo sing such songs as "Simple Gifts" and "I'm on my way to Zion." We have included these songs in the last section of this book and have edited them to illustrate Brother Ricardo's use of embellishment. Because Shaker scribes generally omitted symbols for embellishment, we were not unduly surprised that the unknown scribe of our manuscript copy of "'Tis the gift to be simple" did not indicate them. In running a check on the songs we selected for this collection, we find that the Shaker scribes added grace notes to only fifteen of them.

The dates that Shaker scribes added to a good number of the Shaker songs require close scrutiny. The date might be that of a scribe's inclusion of the song in a manuscript book or of a composer's inspiration to write it. It might also be the year the song was added to a particular manuscript by a visiting Shaker or was imparted to the Shakers by a holy spirit.

From the 1820s through the 1850s the Shakers had been inspired by the presence of founding parents or memories of them, by tunes of English and American songs and ballads, and by the religious revival fervor that swept certain areas of the country. These influences were no longer the driving forces during the latter nineteenth century and after. During this period Shakers began to introduce non-Shaker religious practices such as using the already mentioned standard notation, playing the organ during their religious services, and writing songs based on tunes familiar to members of non-Shaker churches.

Traditionalists among Shakers in the later years felt that the emergence of this "new music" had diminished the role of the "old music" too much. In the preface of the reprint edition of *The Shaker Spiritual*, Daniel Patterson explained his concentration on the older Shaker songs. He mentioned that while he was gathering information for and writing the first edition, he had contact with Sister Mildred Barker at Sabbathday Lake. He reported that the comfort she experienced by his concentration on the old songs deepened his appreciation of the spiritual need of the traditionalists for the old songs.[16]

We have sequenced the selected songs in their original manuscript provenance and page order. The nine manuscripts are labeled A through I in a sequence whereby the two earliest, one dated 1835 and the other 1845, are respectively designated manuscripts A and B. The earlier manuscript contains songs entered in 1835 as well as during the two decades subsequent. Scribes of manuscripts C, D, and E used only the small letteral notation and appear to have entered the bulk of the songs at various times during the second and third quarters of the nineteenth century. Manuscript F has only a few songs that are dated, and those dates fall in the 1870s. Haskell, using his innovative cursive notation system throughout, entered all of the songs in this manuscript. The distinctive handwriting in Manuscript F is a match to that in journals and letters known to have been Haskell's.

The Shaker scribes of manuscripts G, H, and I used round note (standard) notation, a notation that was increasingly in use by the latter nineteenth century. During this time, the use of this notation became much more practical, as Shakers increasingly realized that their diminishing numbers and changing economic status necessitated a changing relationship with the "world's people." The earliest dates in any of these last three manuscripts are those in the 1880s. There are songs in Manuscript I that are dated as late as 1914.

In the last section of the book, "Beyond the Manuscripts," we give four songs not in the manuscripts from among those we heard Brother Ricardo sing at the Shaker Village Work Camp. Three additional songs in this section are variations of versions included in earlier sections of this book. We also include dance instructions that accompany four of the songs.

Acknowledgments

We gratefully acknowledge the publishers and persons listed below for granting permission to quote or paraphrase from published works: Associated University Press (Harold E. Cook, *Shaker Music: A Manifestation of American Folk Culture*, 1973); Peter Count (any materials related to or about the Shakers that were distributed by and bear the imprint of "Shaker Village Work Camp," "Shaker Village Work Group," or "Work Foundation, Inc."); Anna Lomax Chairetakis (John and Alan Lomax, *American Ballad and Folk Songs*, 1934, and *Best Loved American Folk Songs*, 1947); Ann Andrews Kane (Edward D. Andrews, *The Gift to Be Simple*, 1940, rpt. 1967); Daniel W. Patterson, *The Shaker Spiritual*, 1979, rpt. 2001 (also for his letters providing information and encouragement); Kim Seeger (Charles and Ruth Seeger's musical foreword to the Lomaxes' *Best Loved American Folk Songs*, 1947); and Vicki Wells, Rights and Contract Manager at the University of North Carolina Press (George Pullen Jackson, *White Spirituals in the Southern Uplands*, 1933, rpt. 1965).

We certainly could not have made much meaningful progress without the contributions of the following personnel at museum and academic institutions: Dr. Katherine Campbell and Emily Lyle, Department of Celtic and Scottish Studies at the University of Edinburgh, Carol Forbes, Assistant in References Services, National Library of Scotland, Edinburgh, and Robert Kent, Librarian II, General Research Division, New York Public Library, for having been so courteous and patient in providing us with commentary, translations, and suggestions concerning dialect words in "Bonny Wee One"; Jerry V. Grant, Research Director at the Shaker Museum and Library in Old Chatham, New York, for writing the introduction to our book and making it possible for us to have copies of photographs from the library collection—he warmly responded to our many phone calls and visits over the past several years, during which he readily directed us to many appropriate sources and shared with us his own scholarship and enthusiasm; Tommy Hines, Shaker Museum in South Union, Kentucky, for his numerous responses to queries concerning our South Union song manuscript; and Christian Goodwillie, Curator of Collections at Hancock Shaker Village, for responding so readily to our request for photographs, background information on Hancock, and sources related to the Hancock Shakers, and Sally Morse Majewski, Director of Marketing and Public Relations at Hancock Shaker Village, for approving our request to take photographs of various Hancock buildings and extending the courtesy to the inclusion of the sites in this book.

We also owe a debt of appreciation to many individuals in the music field. Barbara Benedict Zimet, college and private consultant and teacher for piano with background in classical, ethnic, and folk music, gave extraordinary amounts of time, energy, and interest to the entire undertaking. Her contributions have been so significant that, without her, the dream of having these songs ready for publication may well have not become a reality. Dr. Joanna Ching-Yun Lee, musicologist, drew on her extensive formal and informal musical training and experience here and abroad to serve as music consultant during the early years of our song editing process. Robert Stuart (Stu) Jamieson, author, folk singer and banjo player, wrote the foreword, showered us with ongoing encouragement, and enjoyed refreshing our recollections of Brother Ricardo Belden's teachings on song and dance.

Offers to contribute other specialized skills came from many different directions. Anthony Cannistra, over many long and late hours, did considerable troubleshooting when song graphic files balked, served as an on-the-scene consultant in converting song graphics, and sequenced the manuscript files. James Kropp aided in the selection of scanner and graphic equipment and stayed on to scan selected songs from the Shaker manuscripts. Steve Sherman generously coordinated and participated in the enhancement of photographs, recreated line drawings, and shared his experiences with manuscript preparation.

Others who offered encouragement and support included Virginia Starke, who read through the manuscript several times, correcting errors and submitting several fruitful suggestions; Leonard Zimet and Mary Ickes, who spent considerable time searching for elusive information on the Web; and Regina Martin-Woodruff, Marianne Sciolino, Eva Wesselmann, and Leslie M. Woodruff, who proofread or shared trips to museums and libraries.

We owe special thanks to Richard M. Abel, Director of the University Press of New England, and Jessica Stevens, Production Editor, for their courteous and much needed assistance, patience, and understanding.

Any errors that may surface in this work are ours and not those of any of the above named persons or institutions.

Introduction: The Shakers

With fewer than a half dozen members at the turn of the twenty-first century, the Shaker Church is the smallest established religious sect in the world. Although small in its number, however, the Shaker faith itself remains strong. As Brother Theodore Johnson wrote in the 1961 introductory issue of *The Shaker Quarterly,* "Despite the vicissitudes which time has worked upon us, the divine truths upon which Shakerism has rested for nearly two hundred years are unchanged and unchangeable." It is those same truths that provide today's Shakers at Sabbathday Lake in Maine with the ability to continue on with great spiritual strength.

Shaker beliefs challenge America's basic values. From the time of their eighteenth-century roots, near Manchester, England, Shakers confronted the Anglican Church to the point that their founder, Ann Lee, was repeatedly jailed. They arrived in the American Colonies in 1774, at the dawn of the Revolutionary War. Turn-the-other-cheek pacifists, they were once again jailed for their religious practices and because they were distrusted as possible British Loyalists.

As a millennial church, one that believes that Christ's return and subsequent thousand-year earthly reign began in the mid-eighteenth century, Shakerism diminishes the promise of the second coming preached by other Christian denominations. Shakers believe that Ann Lee was the messenger who proclaimed the return of the Christ Spirit to mankind. Shakerism further challenges the common male-centered view of God: a Father-Mother God, and Christ in the male and female, dismisses Trinitarianism and creates a gender-balanced deity.

The "world's people" during the early years of Shakerism often viewed the Shaker espousal of the celibate life—no marriage, no sexual relations, and no childbearing—as a threat to the core structure of the American family. The special "families" of Shaker men and women living together as spiritual brothers and sisters forced courts and legislatures to respond to the concerns of the world's people. Court decisions and legislative acts had to address the complicated issues that arose. One such issue concerned spouses and children becoming Shakers over the objection of family members they left behind.

Shakers have always chosen to live outside the common course of the world. They practiced small-"c" communism—a community sharing all things in common—which challenged the new nation's economic system by providing a working alternative to capitalism. They avoided following the fads and fashions that often led men and women to keep up with or outdo their neighbors in styles and quantities of worldly possessions. In doing so the Shakers developed distinctive designs for buildings, clothing, and furnishings that were outside the mainstream style of American design.

The Shakers' persistence and tenacity is worthy of careful examination. The work before us provides the opportunity to look at this fascinating group through their music. For the Shaker, music is an ever-present part of daily life and worship. As important as music is to the Shaker, it is not surprising that the development and use of music parallels the Shakers' history. During their formative years in England and America, the Shakers derived their beliefs from impulses received in spiritual visions. Through revelation, Ann Lee was informed that her followers should listen to their own spiritual gifts. Through revelation, she was informed that the Christ Spirit was again among the peoples of the earth. Ann, like Jesus seventeen centuries earlier, was the vessel through which that spirit flowed. And through revelation, Ann was informed that sexual love stood in the way of living the Christ life. Ann and her followers began to live as celibates, placing brotherly and sisterly love before the relationship of marriage. Many of Ann's followers experienced their own revelations, and all were trying to understand how to incorporate them into their lives.

Shaker worship followed the same course of revelation. Men and women received gifts of songs—melodies without words that were hummed or sung with nonsense syllables. The performance of songs often led to dancing. The dancing was just as unstructured—shaking, jumping, spinning, rolling on the ground, yelping, barking, howling, and speaking in tongues, without concern for or attention to what others in the room were doing. This type of worship continued for nearly two decades. It caused Ann's followers to be called "Shaking Quakers" for the similarity seen in their behavior to that of the early members of the Society of Friends.

Ann Lee died in 1784. Several hundred Americans throughout New England had already united through the beliefs she espoused. In 1787, a group of one hundred were called into "gospel order" and settled in a united community in New Lebanon, New York. This first formal communal gathering in Shaker society created an increased need for order. Who was responsible for what? How would property be held by the community and its members? How would relationships between the sexes by defined?

Several years after Ann's death, Joseph Meacham became the leader of the society. Joseph began to impose regulation through a set of "way-marks." Other groups of Ann's followers—converts "gathered into the faith" during a missionary journey Ann made through New England—were formed into communities that followed the model established at New Lebanon. During this period, Joseph Meacham and his female counterpart, Lucy Wright, brought order to Shaker worship as well. Individual ecstatic shaking and twirling was channeled into choreographed dances. With the introduction of these dances came songs that fit them. Newly gathered communities wanted instruction in the dances and songs, which occurred through visits between communities.

In 1805 there was a "new opening of the gospel" in Kentucky and Ohio that followed missionary efforts made there by the New York Shakers. Hundreds of new Believers gathered into communities there. In 1812 and 1813, the Shakers printed their first hymnal, *Millennial Praises*, in order that multiple copies could be circulated among the nearly twenty Shaker villages that had been established. These new Shakers also needed to learn the dances and songs as they were performed in New Lebanon. In addition to *Millennial Praises*, which provided words without music, the Shakers began to record song melodies in manuscript hymnals using a variety of systems to represent the different notes of the scale. They used traditional round notes and the shape notes of the New England singing schools, but they also devised a unique system of notation created by placing letters that represented notes in a straight line or on a four- or five-line staff. There was great variety in these systems of "letteral notation" and

a greater debate among Shakers on which system was best for adoption by all Shaker communities.

This debate addressed an essential element of Shaker belief—the necessity of "keeping in union" with all other Shakers. In keeping in union, Shakers tried to secure a uniformity and fairness among all members, striving for consistency in rules and regulations, costume, architecture, diet, household furnishings, and worship. In attempting to ensure that Shakers in Maine would sing not only the same words but the same tune, tempo, and pitch as Shakers in Kentucky, a "tone-ometer" was developed to set the pitch of songs and a "mode-ometer" to set the tempo at which they were sung. In the 1840s, Shakers wrote and printed two different musical instruction manuals: *A Short Abridgment of the Rules of Music* was written and printed by Isaac N. Youngs in 1843, and *The Musical Expositor*, written by Russell Haskell, was published in 1847.

By the 1820s, increasing numbers of converts had come to live in Shaker villages, and membership approached four thousand. Converts brought property and provided skills and labor. Shaker communities flourished—buildings were enlarged, business broadened, more land cultivated, and more stock pastured. Success had a price, however. Worldliness crept back into Shaker societies. Individuals began to have more personal belongings, and books from the outside world became too numerous. As more people from outside came to watch the Shakers worship in song and dance, services became more of a performance than a form of worship.

In 1837 a revival began in Shaker communities in New York and spread quickly throughout the Shaker world. Some Shakers began to worship "in the back manner," that is, in the more ecstatic way of the early Shakers. Many Shakers found themselves experiencing increasing numbers of gifts or visions. These came in the form of messages from the spirits of departed Shaker leaders and other beloved members. The messages were received in prose, poetry, pictorial images, and songs—thousands of songs. Those who received these gifts were instructed by angels to record these visions, and they did. The songs were written down by specially appointed scribes. Henry Blinn, a leader at the Shaker village at Canterbury, New Hampshire, recognized the significance of this outpouring of songs and gathered hundreds of them to be published. He had special type cut, and he printed *A Sacred Repository of Hymns* in 1852. This was the first Shaker hymnal printed in letteral notation. The revival period lasted well into the 1850s, dying down as the Civil War approached.

During and after the Civil War, Shaker communities continued to thrive in a temporal manner, but it was clear that fewer and fewer adults were attracted to the Shaker life. For a number of years Shaker membership had been supplemented by orphaned and indentured children. They provided farm and workshop labor and a pool from which the Shakers hoped new adult Shakers would emerge. This was rarely the case, however, and following the Civil War it became clear that the Shakers needed to look elsewhere for adult members.

In the late 1850s, some Shaker villages sent missionaries on a lecture circuit. Lectures and Shaker meetings were held in cities with the hope of attracting new converts. One Shaker, Frederick Evans, went to England to attract converts at lectures he delivered there. In 1871, the Shakers launched a new periodical, *The Shaker*. It was intended to reach a wide audience of spiritual seekers who might unite with the Shakers. They hoped to present themselves as a thoroughly modern and progressive church in the pages of this newspaper. Within a year they began to include Shaker music in each issue. To emphasize the modern aspects of Shakerism—and because few people who lived outside Shaker villages read their letteral notation—songs were published in traditional round-note notation. The introduction of round notes and the use of pianos and organs during singing practice and worship in the early 1870s eventually led to the singing of Shaker songs in parts. (Previously, almost all Shaker music was sung without musical accompaniment and with a single melody line for all of the singers.) Songs written with round notes were also gathered into several hymnals, including *Shaker Music*, published in 1884, and *Original Shaker Music*, published in 1893. Except for some uniquely Shaker language, they could easily be mistaken for a Methodist or Baptist hymnal of the same period.

Worship during the last decade of the nineteenth century reflected the aging Shaker population. Dances were replaced with marches—processions of Shakers two, four, six, and eight abreast—around the meetinghouse sanctuary. The quick dances in choreographed patterns were disappearing—no more circle dances, hollow squares, and square order shuf-

fles. Although the older songs were sometimes renovated and included in new hymnals, and some Shakers lobbied to return to them for worship, they were retired from use during the second quarter of the twentieth century. At the same time, some Shaker communities chose to worship outside the community in neighboring churches or to invite local pastors and priests to come to their villages to minister to them. Hymns from other Christian churches became some of the Shakers' worship music.

In the 1950s, ethnomusicologist Daniel W. Patterson's work on Shaker music led him to form relationships with Shakers at Hancock, Massachusetts, Canterbury, New Hampshire, and Sabbathday Lake, Maine. At Sabbathday Lake he met Sister R. Mildred Barker, from whom he learned many of the old Shaker songs that had been passed down to her through oral tradition. In turn, Patterson's enthusiasm rekindled a desire in that Shaker village to renew the use of older Shaker songs. As has been the case throughout Shaker history, the spiritual and the musical remain inseparable. The Shakers at Sabbathday Lake were returning to an older, more traditional form of Shaker worship as they learned the old Shaker songs.

Today at Sabbathday Lake, music remains an essential part of Shaker worship. Set songs, usually selected and sung from one of the round-note hymnals, are used as a call to worship. When individual testimonies and reflections on scriptures occur in meeting, many of the older songs garnered from the community's memory, oral tradition, manuscripts, and printed hymnals are used to punctuate testimonies or to give comfort and support to worshipers. Shakers today hold hundreds of songs in their oral tradition, and as many as ten thousand more are recorded in manuscript and printed hymnals. It is a tremendously rich resource for students of music and, more importantly, for spiritual seekers.

JERRY GRANT
Director of Research
Shaker Museum and Library, Old Chatham, New York

Notes on Transcribing and Editing:
Process and Rationale

The decision to select and transcribe songs from the original manuscripts immediately raised the question of how best to protect the physical integrity of the nine manuscripts. To avoid the repeated page-turning that a lengthy selection and transcription process would require, we opted to photocopy the manuscripts in an archival-approved fashion.

Certain songs "jumped off the pages" during the initial sight-reading stage. We chose, for the most part, to give priority to songs that had not yet been published and to variations of some already published. Other influences included the auditory appeal of tune and text and the singularity of the background and music notation of the songs under consideration.

The song numbers assigned to the twenty scanned manuscript songs in this section match the numbers of their transcript and edited counterparts that appear in later sections of this book. These twenty facsimile songs offer the reader an opportunity to compare the handwritten songs in the original manuscripts with our transcript and edited copies. The transcript copies, positioned on the lefthand pages, differ from the original Shaker songs in that we have placed the notes on a staff and used standard notation to do so. Conversely, we have let stand omission of bars, tempo, time, signatures, and text-note alignment when such omissions occur in the manuscripts. The edited formats of all songs in sections one through nine appear on the righthand pages.

Names of persons, communities, dates, or combinations thereof in the transcript copies appear in locations approximating those of the facsimile copies. Compare, for instance, the locations of this identifying information in A 9, "I love Gods way," with the location of the same addenda in D 58, "We're happy and free." On the other hand, we have made no attempt to reproduce the various decorative designs the Shaker scribes sometimes placed at the beginning of their songs, nor have we reproduced the squiggles and unique sequence of vertical lines of descending lengths found at the end of many songs, as in the facsimile copy of E 73, "Lodle lo lodle lodle lo."

The majority of the twenty songs shown here in facsimile is among the many that we have transposed into keys more suitable for average voice range. Only four of the facsimile copies—D 56, "Trust in the Lord," D 58, "We're happy and free," D 63, "We are strong" and E 73 (Lodle lo lodle lodle lo)—retain their original keys in their edited formats.

Barbara Zimet was especially helpful when we were ready to harmonize the edited versions of the songs. She stressed the advantage of adding chord inversion notation when appropriate instead of merely identifying the chord. "C/E," for example, means an inverted C chord in which E is the bottom note of the chord. Music teachers, individual performers, and choral or instrumental groups should find that these additions and clarifications make the songs more readily usable. Chords did not seem to be appropriate for the chantlike B 35, "The Saviour's Universal Prayer," and C 47, "In de shiny Muders mansion."

Old-style variant spellings and, occasionally, a misspelling appear in a few songs in both the following facsimile copies and the left-page transcript copies later in the book. We have corrected or updated them in the edited versions on the right pages. Harold Cook, aware of the spelling variants in Shaker songs, wrote:

> Colloquial usage and phonetic spelling found so frequently in these handwritten pages from 1800 on are not peculiar to the Shakers, but, it must be remembered, existed practically everywhere in the rural regions of our country at the time. An expanding and ever-shifting frontier, with few schools and limited book learning, made these unorthodox constructions and spellings the rule rather than the exception.[1]

Songs having spelling variations include A 34, "Like a little busy bee," D 56, "Trust in the Lord," D 58, "We're happy

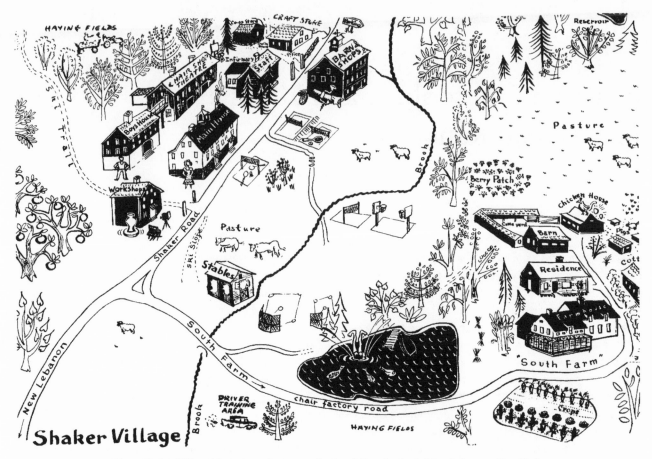

Fig. 1. Shaker Village Work Camp layout on the South Family site in New Lebanon, New York.
COURTESY PETER COUNT.

and free," D 63, "We are strong in the Lord," and D 65, "Hark! The merry Bells are ringing." For specific examples of spelling variations, see the introduction to the Manuscript D collection of songs.

Creating tentative edited versions of the songs underscored the need for their review by music professionals who had recognized expertise in music, including specific knowledge of and experience in folk and religious music. When Joanna Lee had to leave to meet overseas commitments, Barbara Zimet stayed on for several years, even up to the eve of publication. She worked with us through many sessions of exhausting but necessary editing, re-editing, and consultations.

A large number of songs in the Shaker manuscripts have no titles. The opening phrase serves as the title of the edited version of any such song. Compare C 46, "Bonny Wee One," which has a title assigned by the Shaker scribe or composer, and the song that immediately follows it, C 47, "In de shiny Muder's mansion," which has no title in the manuscript. In the latter case, we selected the first phrase of the song as the title and capitalized only the first word and any additional word that may have been capitalized by the Shaker scribe.

Five facsimile songs—A 25, "Round Dance," C 46, "Bonny Wee One," C 51, "Earthly pleasures I will leave," E 73, "Lodle lo lodle lodle lo," and F 88, "I will praise the Lord"—either have no text at all or have text in only some measures. The Shakers sang these "noted" (wordless) songs or measures by inserting vocables, that is, syllables having specific sounds but no meaning.

For the convenience of singers today, we have inserted Shaker vocables into the edited versions wherever text is nonexistent in the manuscripts. Because the Shakers did not sanction accompaniment by musical instruments until late in the nineteenth century, vocables were essential in singing such wordless tunes as the early solemn songs. Even when Shakers began to dance and march in an orderly fashion, some new tunes were wordless in part or in their entirety and required the use of vocables. The closest parallel to such usage is the current practice of singing *tra-la-la* or *la-dee-da* or even humming when words are missing or memory fails.

The edited version of each song has a tempo designation. In assigning tempos, we have been guided by a variety of sources, including the few remaining Shakers who were still residing at Hancock during the late 1940s and early 1950s. Other guides to tempo have been Shaker tempo designations on some of the songs, the original works of Youngs and Haskell, books on Shaker music by Andrews, Cook, and Patterson, recordings and collections, recently published song collections, interviews with folk musician Stu Jamieson, inquiries to Jerry Grant, director of research at the Shaker Library in Old Chatham, and our own experience. Barbara Zimet spent a great deal of time with us, singing, playing accompaniments, and listening to tapes of Shaker songs, in order to arrive at what we hope is a workable tempo for each song.

Eighteen of the facsimile songs, detailed below, posed more editing dilemmas than did most any other song.

A 1, "O how I do love good Believers." Neither Isaac Youngs, who wrote or contributed the song, nor Harvey Eades, the scribe, inserted repeat marks for it. We chose not to interpret this as an error in notation. We felt that adding repeats would interrupt the lovely flow of text and music that is present throughout the song.

We have not interpreted the heavy black lines that appear at the top end of the D letteral notes in "O how I do love good Believers" as flags. The flags on linear letteral notation songs in this manuscript are slanted and do not touch the letteral notes. Perhaps a recalcitrant pen, dipped in too much ink, created a problem in penmanship. Furthermore, interpreting these D's as flagged notes violates the rhythm of the song.

A 3, "O Come each lovely Child of grace." This is one of the few in our selection that uses the Shaker repeat symbol ":S:" to designate a section repeat. We changed the key of this song from C to D, a more appropriate singing range. Knowing that "quick" and "gift" songs tend to repeat in both parts and that Shaker scribes sometimes neglected to indicate repeats, we added a repeat sign in the second section of the song.

A 9, "I love God's way." We changed bar lines to fit the rhythm of the text. Every text line in the manuscript copy seems to start with a pick-up note. In measure one, staff one, we changed the bar line so that measure one would have the same kind of pick-up as measure five in staff two. Anyone who feels comfortable with each line of text beginning on a downbeat, as in the manuscript, should certainly feel free to sing it that way.

A 25, "Round Dance." In this song, the text is recorded *beneath* the notes, which are entered in small letteral notation. This makes the song unusual, in that typically the songs using small letteral notation in our manuscripts place the text *over* each music notation area. Note also that there are eight wordless measures at the end of the song requiring the insertion of vocables.

B 35, "The Saviour's Universal Prayer." We have retained the many meter changes that occur in the manuscript copy of this song.

E 73, "(Lodle lo lodle lodle lo)." Because this song has no title or text in the manuscript, we have used vocables for a title in the edit version. We have placed the title in parentheses because the original had no text that could be used as a title.

C 52, "We are all coming home." The scribe added a stemless note in measure two. Rather than delete what appears to be an error, we have converted the stemless note into a grace note in the edited copy. We made some changes in note values and in bar placement for consistency of meter.

D 56, "Trust in the Lord," and *G 111, "I love to commune with the angels."* We moved bars in the edited versions of both songs to better match the music to the accents and rhythms of the texts. For example, the bars in the edited format of "Trust in the Lord" are in what had been mid-measure positions in the Shaker manuscript. The measure change that we made in the first two staffs of "I love to commune with the angels" corrected errors of omission in the original.

We changed the duration of some notes in the edited formats of the following songs to make them easier to sing:

A 25, "Round Dance." Even though it is not immediately clear how to correctly interpret the last note in the first section, we changed its value and made it part of the first ending.

A 34, "Like a little busy bee," F 88, "I will praise the Lord," and F 100, "My soul loves to walk." We converted sixteenth notes to eighth notes to allow for greater ease in reading and singing the text.

C 46, "Bonny Wee One." We made the note values in the last staff match the note values of the preceding staff.

C 51, "Earthly pleasures I will leave." We insured that each measure contains two full beats.

D 57, "Sowing the seed of the Springtime." We better matched the music to the rhythm of the text.

D 65, "Hark! The merry Bells are ringing." The $\frac{2}{4}$ meter required rhythmic adjustment.

The facsimile copy and our transcription copy of H 112, "Behold what wonders now we see," clearly show that the scribe or composer penned an E as the last note in the last measure. When we edited the song, we assumed, however, that the scribe or composer intended the last note to be an F.

Facsimiles of Selected Songs

1. O how I do love good Believers
MS A - p. 1

c|cagaca|gea gg|cdedcd|edc|g·| ⸲ cag|eg g cde|·ge gec|deddcc|(c||c|

cdegeg| age |ge|geddca|cdc|ga|cdcagg|edc ge|gedſed|dcd ⸲c·||||

O how I do love good Believers in truth,
Like trees firmly rooted they bear precious fruit!
Whose souls are united in heavenly love,
Whose faces are set to the mansions above.—
I want nothing greater than union with them—
This pure golden treasure this heavenly gem!—
My cross to the last I will ever maintain
That with Mothers Children the prize I may gain.

I. N. Y. _____ Isaac N. Youngs

3. O Come each lovely Child of grace
MS A - p. 5

O Come each lovely Child of grace
Who stand on Zions holy ground,
And let our love & thankfulness,
In everlasting praise resound;
For we have found a precious store
Of royal gems & glorious things;
Then we'll rejoice forever more
In loud hosannahs to our Kings.
J. N. L. ~   Isaac N young —

I love Gods way I surely do

And I do mean to keep it too

And daily labor to increase

That my abode may be in peace

All my desire is to improve

That I may dwell in perfect love

And I am sure in doing this

That I shall reign in endless bliss.

WVliet- N.Y.
June 2. 1835

N. Wells.

25. "Round Dance"
MS A - p. 163

Round Dance

There's nothing on the earth to bind us

While with saints we are uniting

Lo! we leave the world behind us

Angels are inviting.

H. L. Eades.
S Union

34. Like a little busy bee
MS A - p. 256

Like a little buisy bee

I'll fly around & gather honey

From every pretty flower

Which grow in zions bower

Come every buisy bee

Ye may freely share with me

O' it is a pretty treasure

From our hooly Mother

South Union   H.G.

35. "The Saviour's Universal Prayer"
MS B - pp. 33 - 34

The Saviour's Universal Prayer

Our Father, who art in Heaven
hallowed be thy name, thy kingdom
come, thy will be done on earth as
it is done in Heaven. Give us this
day our daily bread, and forgive
us our debts as we forgive our debtors,
Leave us not in temptation but
deliver us from evil, for thine is the
kingdom, the glory and power forever
more Amen.

46. "Bonny Wee One"
MS C - p. 28

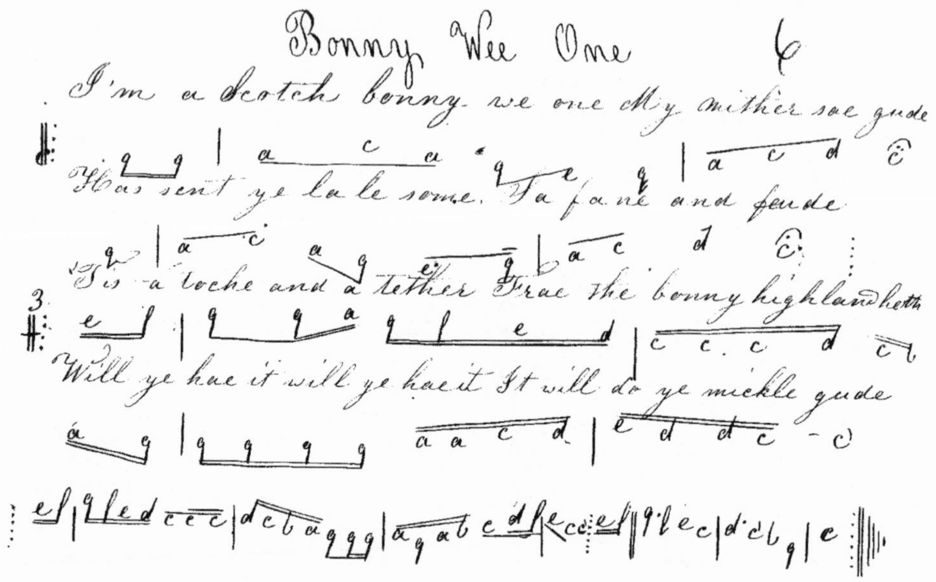

47. In de shiny Muder's mansion
MS C - p. 28

In de shiny Muders mansion me
bow me soul down low   From me Muder

Me nebel nebei will depart

For me   Muder say dat me belong

In de shiny heabens above

51. Earthly pleasures I will leave

MS C - p. 81

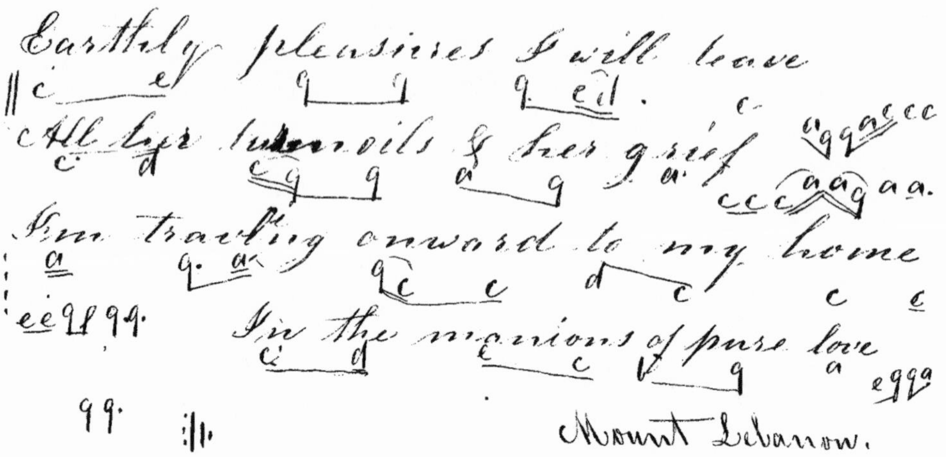
Earthly pleasures I will leave

All her toils & her grief

I'm trav'ling onward to my home

In the mansions of pure love

Mount Lebanon.

52. We are all coming home
MS C - p. 89

56. Trust in the Lord
MS D - p. 49

49

Trust in the Lord His will be done
Tho the tempest rages & the storm comes down
He will guide our Barque O'er the billows high
And land us safely over there bye & bye.
As a guide thro the dark His power has been
To the Sercher for truth he will lend a hand
A helper to those who will help themselves
And work for the spread of the truth upon earth

Harvard April 22. 1894

Andrew Barrill

57. Sowing the seed of the Springtime
MS D - p. 59

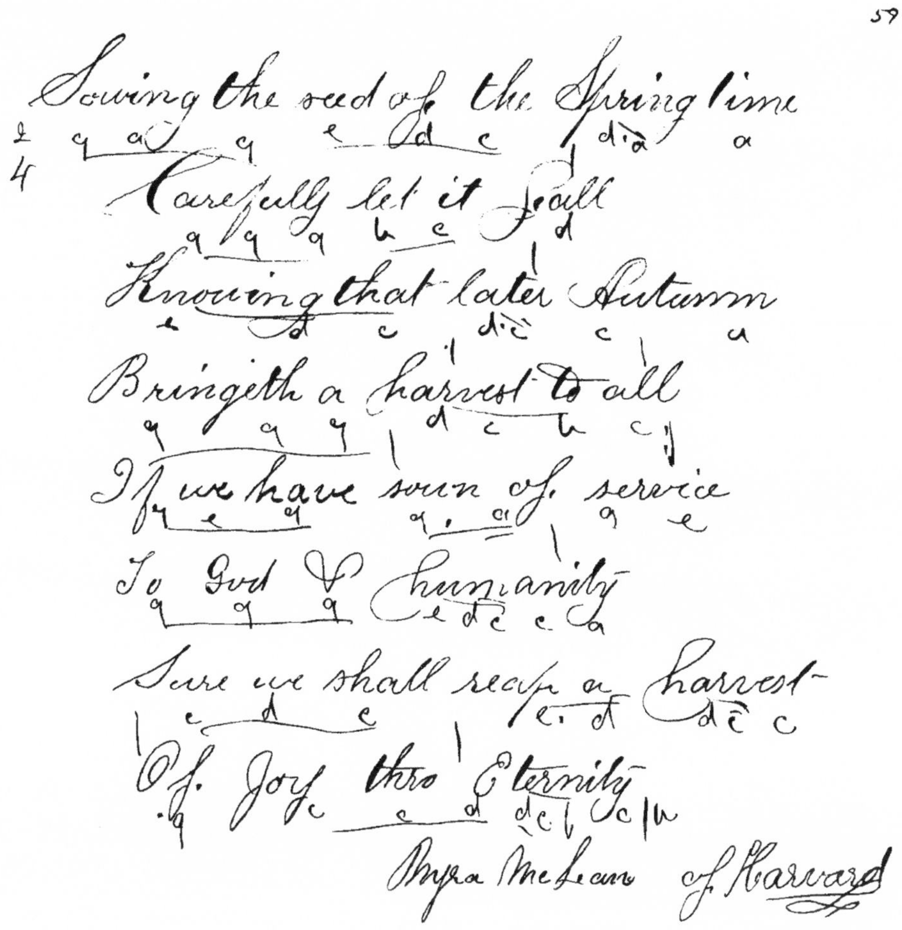
59

Sowing the seed of the Springtime
Carefully let it fall
Knowing that later Autumn
Bringeth a harvest to all
If we have sown of service
To God & humanity
Sure we shall reap a harvest
Of joy thro' Eternity

Myra McLean of Harvard

58. We're happy and free
MS D - p. 73

73

We're happy & free & no Powers that be
Can hinder our Progress to heaven
We're upward bound where sin is not found
Our lives unto God are given
So brethern & sisters we'll journey along
To reach that heaven of Glory
And when we are there in that region so fair
We'll repeat to the Angels our story

1898

Enfield North Family

63. We are strong in the Lord
MS D - p. 118

118

We are strong in the Lord in his might
For his cause we're a patient band
The truth is our Citadel of strength
Where conquering armies round us stand
We are strong we are strong
In the conquest of right over wrong
In the Battle of life we will triumph
And shout we are strong we are strong

No darkness of doubt shall enshroud
Nor fear tho our foes assail
The truth is our everlasting choice
In its conquering power will prevail
We are strong

65. Hark! The merry Bells are ringing
MS D - p. 132

132

Hark the merry Bells are ringing
While we tarry here below
Hear the little Bells are ringing
Ringing ringing ever more
They are calling us togeather
Into Union & sweet Love
Where to love & bless each other
As the Angels do above

White Water

73. (Lodle lo lodle lodle lo)
MS E - p. 169

88. I will praise the Lord
MS F - p. 33

100. My soul loves to walk
MS F - p. 69

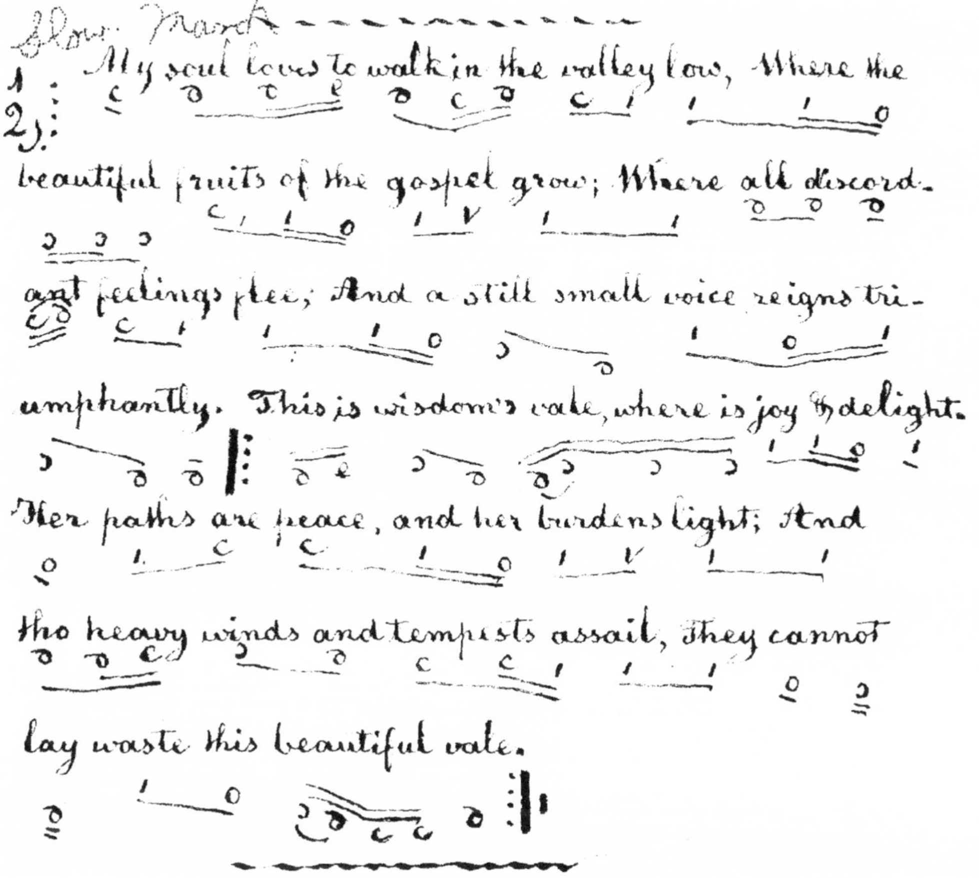

111. I love to commune with the angels
MS G - p. 141

112. Behold what wonders now we see
MS H - p. 13

A *Shaker* Musical Legacy

1

Manuscript A

"A Collection of Verses"

The inscription on the title page of this 1835 manuscript reads "A Collection of Verses by the Singers of South Union, Ky. April 4, 1835. H. L. E." The initials are those of Harvey L. Eades, a Shaker musician at South Union who, along with others in that community, adopted linear letteral notation for a time. Usually using bars but no staff lines, this notation is characterized by tightly written notes placed linearly at the top of the page, with the text set off as a separate unit further down the page. These notes sometimes made it very difficult to distinguish between "C notes" and "E notes" when either would be musically acceptable. Very short horizontal lines positioned above or below a note indicate an upward or downward direction for the note. The transcriber needs to take great care not to interpret these lines as note flags or as wayward pen strokes. The absence of such a line means that the note remains at the same horizontal position as the previous note. Examples of Eades linear letteral notation appear in the following Manuscript A facsimile songs from the preceding section: 1, "O how I do love good Believers," 3, "O Come each lovely Child of grace," 9, "I love God's way," and 34, "Like a little busy bee."

Linear letteral notation did not gain favor in communities other than South Union, where it reached its high point at the time songs were being recorded in the first segment of this manuscript. As time went on, scribes interspersed linear letteral notation with the more widely accepted small letteral notation on subsequent pages. Eades's most well-known musician contemporaries, Isaac Youngs and Russel Haskell, both used small letteral notation throughout each of their treatises on Shaker music.[1]

Several specimens of handwriting, different forms of mu-

sical notation, and songs with dates extending from 1835 to the 1850s characterize the thirty-four songs we culled from this manuscript. Occasionally a song title specifically identifies the song as a quick song, which is also known as a "standing" or an "extra" song. When Daniel Patterson examined this manuscript, it was still in the possession of Jerry Count at New Lebanon. Patterson identified the bulk of the songs as extra songs, that is, one-stanza songs used during rest sessions between dances, in worship, in work situations, and on special occasions.[2] A few songs bear as titles the kinds of dances to be performed with titles such as "March" or "Round Dance." The latter is a later form of the Shaker circular dance and was more structured than the earliest of the circular quick dances.

"O freedom, lovely in my eyes" is the only song in this manuscript—in fact, in the entire collection—in which the shape-note system was used (fig. 2). Early music schools in New England, New York, and adjacent states used this notation, but it fell from favor with the introduction of more sophisticated notation forms from Europe. People along the frontier and in the south readily adopted the friendlier shape-note notation and held on to it for decades. Even today, shape-note societies throughout the United States keep shape-note songbooks in print and use them in their singing sessions. Over the years, shape notes have been known by a variety of names including buckwheat, patent, and character.

In their often reprinted treatise *The Easy Instructor,* William Little and William Smith expounded on a shape-note system using only four shapes—triangle, circle, square, and diamond—to represent faw, sol, law, and the lead tone, me.

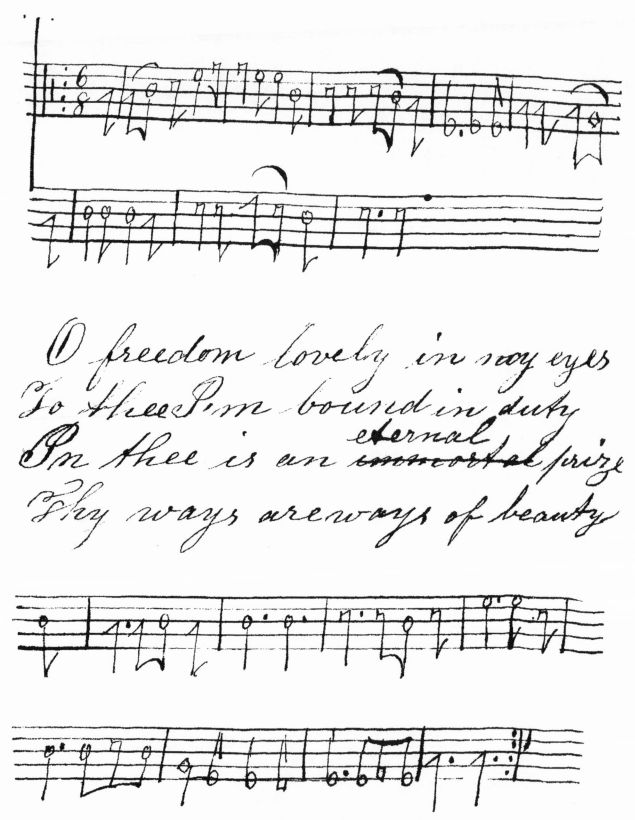

O freedom lovely in my eyes
To thee I'm bound in duty
On thee is an ~~immortal~~ eternal prize
Thy ways are ways of beauty

Fig. 2. "O freedom lovely in my eyes." Shape note notation (Manuscript A).

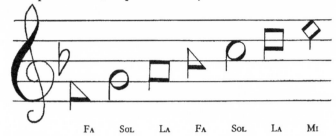

Fa   Sol   La   Fa   Sol   La   Mi

Fig. 3. Shape note notation. REPRINTED FROM GEORGE PULLEN JACKSON, *White Spirituals in the Southern Uplands*, 1933, 1965, P. 14.

The repeat of "faw sol law" in the scale recognizes that B♭CD and FGA each have the same intervals (fig. 3).

By 1818, Shakers at Watervliet had adopted the system and had begun to modify the appearance of the notes. For example, they altered note heads that were less than a half note in value by outlining them rather than filling them in with ink as Little and Smith had done. Patterson found that the Shaker scribes at Watervliet used a short horizontal line on the stem of half notes to avoid confusing them with their newly outlined quarter notes.[3] Yet in "O freedom, lovely in my eyes," the scribe at South Union made a different distinction. Instead of adding horizontal lines across the stems of half notes, he drew flags on the quarter and eighth notes (fig.3). In his study of eight hundred song manuscripts, Patterson unearthed a dozen manuscripts—and adds "and others"—that contain one or more songs in which shape notes appear.[4]

The abundance of gift songs in this manuscript is a testimony to the outpouring of such songs during the 1837–1847 period of spirit manifestation with which this manuscript coincided. Not all gift songs came from the spirit of Mother Ann Lee or from other spirits who had been Shakers in life. The Shakers believed, interestingly, that those who had not been Shakers as living persons could become Shakers as spirits, therefore sanctioned to offer gifts.

Gift songs continued to appear well after the prolific outpouring of gift songs during the pre–Civil War period of spirit manifestation. Brother Ricardo recalled that "gift songs were given to a brother or sister at any hour of the day or night, when the spirit came to bring them [i.e., the songs]. I have known them to be given in the daytime while the brethren and sisters were at work, but most of them were given in the quiet hours of the night."[5]

Although many such songs were gifts themselves, other gift songs specifically name the nature of the spirit gifts. The last five of the thirty-four songs we selected from this manuscript—"A Laughing Song," "I have a little trumpet," "Drink ye of Mother's wine," "Little children," and "Like a little busy bee"—are examples of this type of gift song. Each of these songs identifies the giver of the gift (love, wine, a trumpet, or honey) as "Mother," meaning Ann Lee. "A Laughing Song," "Drink ye of Mother's wine," and "Little children" also invite the Shakers to drink wine in order to experience a high degree of religious ecstasy while singing and dancing. Actually, early Shakers did make and use alcoholic beverages, but, in the later decades of the nineteenth century, they became increasingly censorious toward the use of alcohol. Eyewitnesses reported that the wine offered at the mountain meetings (see the introduction to section two) was actually invisible and spiritual.

The focal point of the manuscript, of course, is its song collection, but inscriptions on the front and back flyleaves also merit attention, in that they shed some light on the fate of the manuscript during the 1890s. The first of the two notations appearing immediately after the title page is "This book was given to me by Betsey Smith of South Union Kentucky in Aug 1894. She now being 80 years of age. At one time she was Eldress of the Center Family and a no of years minister in the order of Shakers at South Union Ky—A. O. Packard South Union Ky." The second notation reads "Eldress Betsey Smith departed this life on the 28 of Feby 1896 at South Union Kentucky, aged 82 years Having been in the Shaker Order since she was 11 years of age & minister in the Order 45 years." The Packard name reappears on the last page: "Mr Ralph Packard Dixon Ill. Lin Co, A O Packard Eddy N. Mexico Jany 23*d* 1897" (fig. 4).

This information stimulates a strong desire to learn more. What was the itinerary for the manuscript during the early decades of the twentieth century? How did it end up at Hancock? Was the manuscript ever returned to South Union before it closed in 1922? If it was returned to the South Union community, did someone there give it as a gift to a visiting Shaker from New Lebanon or Hancock? Did the two remaining Shakers at South Union serve as a means of trans-

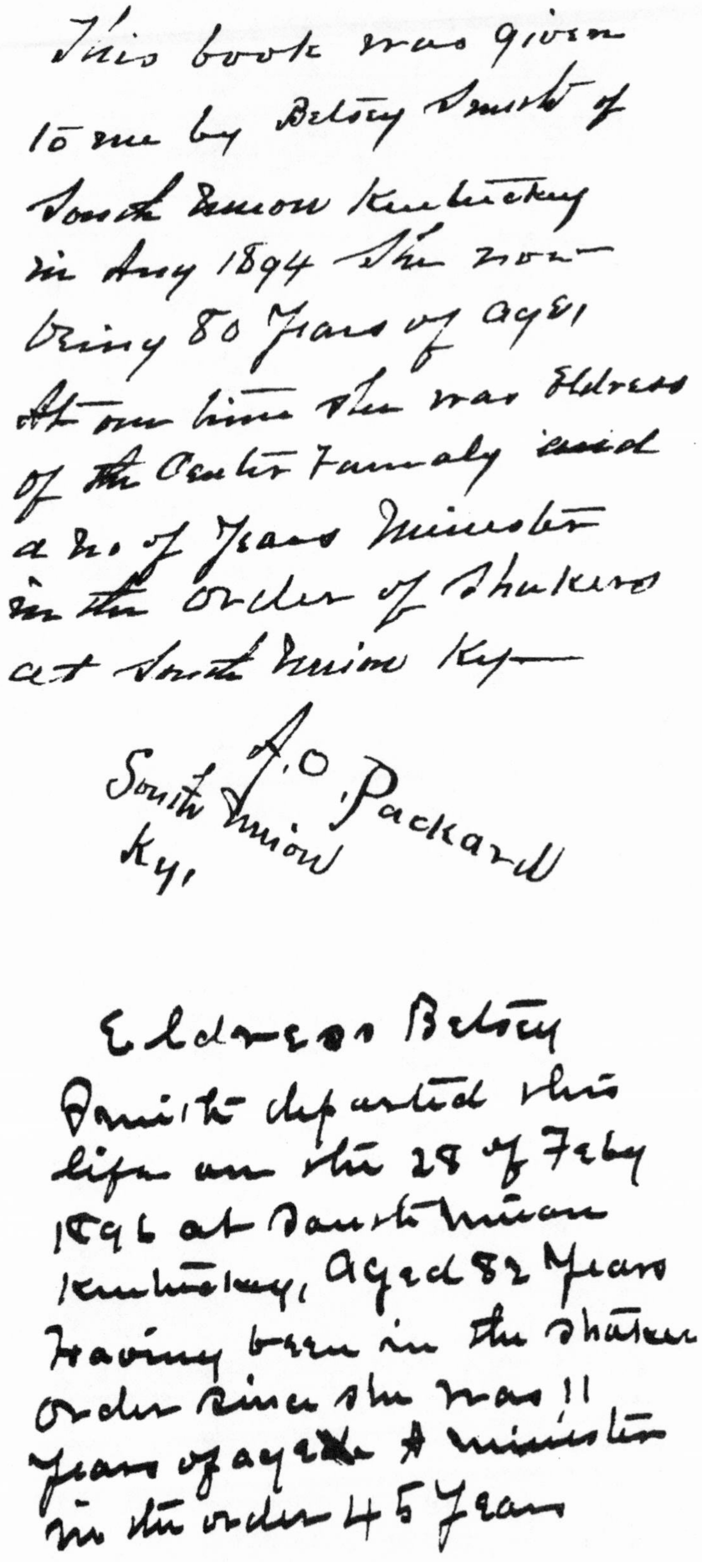

*This book was given
to me by Betsey Smith of
South Union Kentucky
in Aug 1894 She now
being 80 Years of age.
At one time she was Eldress
of the Center Family and
a no. of Years Minister
in the order of Shakers
at South Union Ky —*

A. O. Packard
South Union
Ky,

*Eldress Betsey
Smith departed this
life on the 28 of Feby
1896 at South Union
Kentucky, Aged 82 Years
Having been in the Shaker
order since she was 11
Years of age & a minister
in the order 45 Years*

Fig. 4. Flyleaf inscriptions in Manuscript A, signed by A. O. Packard.

fer when they were taken to the New Lebanon community in 1922? Did the manuscript, if taken to New Lebanon, arrive at Hancock when New Lebanon closed in 1947? Did a member or associate of the Packard family give it directly to the New Lebanon or Hancock communities?

Both Julia Neal, in *The Kentucky Shakers,* and Stephen Stein, in *The Shaker Experience in America,* include engrossing details about the closing of the South Union community, but they do not refer to the fate of any of the South Union song manuscripts.[6] In response to our inquiry about this matter, Tommy Hines, researcher at the South Union Shaker Museum, wrote "There were, of course, many other visits to the east from Kentucky as well. Eldress Jane Cowan visited Canterbury in the 1870s. Eades made a number of visits; Elder Benjamin Seth Youngs brought South Union things with him when he returned east about 1840."[7]

This small South Union manuscript, in which the first song was entered eighty-seven years before South Union closed, remains a silent reminder of a once vibrant community.

MS SV–A/**SU–2** p. 1

O how I do love good Believers in truth,
Like trees firmly rooted they bear precious fruit!
Whose souls are united in heavenly love,
Whose faces are set to the mansions above. −
I want nothing greater than union with them −
This pure golden treasure this heavenly gem!
My cross to the last I'll ever maintain
That with Mothers Children The prize I may gain.

N. L. ‒‒‒‒‒‒‒‒‒   *Isaac N. Youngs*

O how I do love good Believers

Isaac N. Youngs
New Lebanon, New York

MS SV–A/**SU–2** p. 2

I have a little Love!
A little love, a little love!
O here it is! O here it is!
Will you partake?
Will you partake?
'Tis pure & clean from Mother Ann –
If you'll partake She says you can.

Abm. Perkins
North Enfield
N. Hampshire

I have a little Love!

Abraham Perkins
North Enfield, New Hampshire

MS SV-A/**SU-2** p. 5

: **S** :

O Come each lovely Child of grace
Who stand on Zions holy ground,
And let our love & thankfulness,
In everlasting praise resound;
For we have found a precious store
Of royal gems & glorious things;
Then we'll rejoice for evermore
In loud hozannahs to our Kings.

N.L. ---

Isaac N. Youngs ____

O Come each lovely Child of grace

Isaac N. Youngs
New Lebanon, New York

Joyfully (♩=72)

O___ Come each love – ly Child of grace Who stands on Zi-on's ho-ly ground, And let our_ love and thank-ful-ness, In ev – er – last – ing praise re – sound.___ For we have found a pre – cious store Of roy – al gems and glo – ri – ous things; Then we'll re – joice for ev – er more In loud ho-san-nahs to our King(s).

MS SV–A/**SU–2** p. 15

Let music sound & echo round _
Tune up ye pleasant harpers _
Mount Zions songs truly belong
To Mothers Sons & Daughters.
Her lovely hand doth lead the Band,
While forward we're advancing __
Along the way the Virgins play
With music and with dancing.

N. L.   –––––––   *Jane Smith*

Let music sound and echo 'round

Jane Smith
New Lebanon, New York

MS SV-A/**SU-2** p. 20

I'm looking round about to see,
(As doth the little honey Bee
To find a sweet delicious flow'r)
Whence I can draw some life and pow'r
O here it is I've found it nigh,
And round about it I will fly _
'Tis to my taste so very sweet
I will invite you all to eat.

Enfield, N. H.

I'm looking 'round about to see

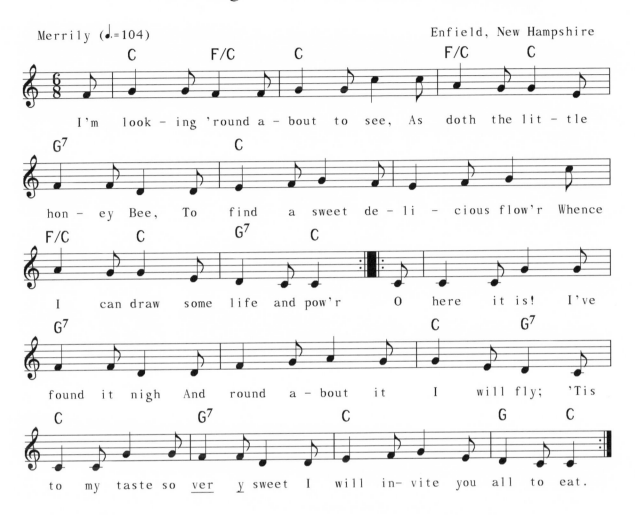

Merrily (♩.=104)   Enfield, New Hampshire

I'm look-ing 'round a-bout to see, As doth the lit-tle hon-ey Bee, To find a sweet de-li-cious flow'r Whence I can draw some life and pow'r O here it is! I've found it nigh And round a-bout it I will fly; 'Tis to my taste so ver-y sweet I will in-vite you all to eat.

MS SV-A/**SU-2** p. 21

:S:

I am determined to be free,
No carnal ties shall hinder me;
For Mothers gospel I can see,
Is safety to rely on.____
All those who keep her righeous laws
And bear their cross without a pause,
Do flourish like a sharon rose,
Upon the Mount of Zion.

N. L. ---------

Olive Fairbanks

I am determined to be free

Olive Fairbanks
New Lebanon, New York

MS SV-A/**SU-2** p. 28

Come let us all now be alive
And keep the gifts of Heaven,
It will our spirits all revive
And we will be good Children;
Then we will love and be belov'd,
All in one spirit growing.
And all our bands will be remov'd
And we together flowing.

S. U. ~~~~~~~~~~~~~~   I . R.Eades

Come let us all now be alive

I. R. Eades
South Union, Kentucky

MS SV–A/**SU–2** p. 35

I will labor to be free;
For love & for simplicity. ___
I will labor to be low,
So at the work I freely go.

S. U.   ~~~~~   *Keturah Harrison*

Note __ every other strain of the above tune is sung without words ___ they being applied to the first. _____

I will labor to be free

Keturah Harrison
South Union, Kentucky

MS SV–A/**SU–2** p. 45

I love Gods way I surely do
And I do mean to keep it too
And daily labor to increase
That my abode may be in peace
All my desire is to improve
That I may dwell in perfect love
And I am sure in doing this
That I shall reign in endless bliss.

W–vliet – N. Y
June 2, 1835

N. Wells.

I love God's way

N. Wells
Watervliet, New York, June 2, 1835

With assurance (♩.=80–92)

I _____ love God's way; I sure - ly do, And I__ do mean to keep it, too, And_ dai - ly la - bor to in-crease That my__ a - bode may be in peace.__ I _____ be in peace._____ All_____ my de - sire is to__ im - prove That I may dwell in per - fect love And____ I am sure in do - ing this That I____ shall reign in end - less bliss,_____ All____ end - less bliss,_____

I will be free I'll not be bound
Haughty self it shall come down
A wicked nature I will fight.
I'll have a sword that's keen & bright.

I will be free, I'll not be bound

With determination (♩=120)

I will be free, I'll not be bound;
Haugh - ty self it shall come down.
A wick-ed na - ture I will fight;
I'll have a sword that's keen and bright.

MS SV-A/**SU-2** p. 53

M   Doolittle _____

Lovely souls march along
To the holy mountain
Let us drink our fill of love
At the flowing fountain. ___
Those who make it their employ
To be meek & lowly
They shall feast on endless joy
With the pure & holy.

June 23
1835

Isaac N. Youngs.
New Lebanon.

Lovely souls march along

M. Doolittle
Briskly (♩=112)

Isaac N. Youngs
New Lebanon, New York, June 23, 1835

Love - ly souls march a - long To the ho - ly__
moun - tain; Let us drink our_ fill of love
At the flow - ing foun - tain. Those who make it__
their em - ploy To be meek and_ low - ly,
They shall feast on__ end- less joy with the pure and ho - ly.

– 1 2 –

M a r c h

MS SV–A/**SU-2** p. 64

Canterbury. N. H.

March

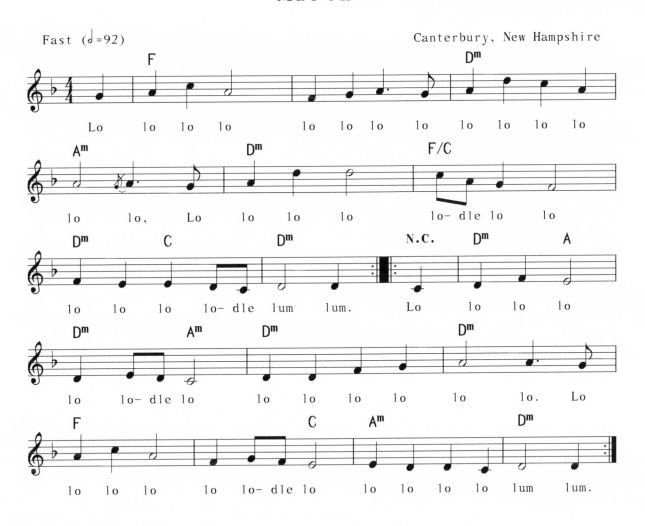

MS SV–A/**SU–2** p. 68

In this new and living way
How I love to skip and play
Join'd in songs of heavenly mirth
Bound for Zion while on earth
Seeking an immortal prize
With the virgins pure and wise
Leaving all that is impure.
For a treasure firm and sure.

N. L.~~___

Henry De Witt's
. . . .

In this new and living way

Henry DeWitt
New Lebanon, New York

Cheerfully (♩=60)

In this new and liv- ing way How I love to skip and play;

Join'd in songs of heav'n- ly mirth, Bound for Zi- on while on earth;

Seek- ing an im – mor-tal prize With the vir- gins pure and wise;

Leav- ing all that is im – pure For a trea- sure firm and sure.

MS SV–A/**SU–2** p. 69

Mary An Doolittle

May we now in pure devotion
March with joy the Heavenly road
Thro' the fields of tribulation
We can view the blest abode
Where the righteous dwell forever
Free from sorrow grief or pain
O my soul press on with vigor
That you may this Kindom gain.

copied by H. DeWitt
New Lebanon, 1835

Julia Doolittle's

May we now in pure devotion

Julia Doolittle
With a pulse (♩.=92)

Mary A. Doolittle
Copied by H. DeWitt, New Lebanon, N.Y. 1835

May we now in pure de - vo - tion March with joy_ the

Heaven-ly road. Thro' the fields of tri - bu - la - tion

We can view the blest a - bode. Where the right - eous

dwell for - ev - er, Free from sor - row, grief, or pain,

O my soul press on with vig - or That you may this King- dom gain.

MS SV-A/**SU-2** p. 71

Come let us play and skip around
Let us be in motion
Alive in evry gift be found
In this pure devotion.
We surely know it is the way
To be meek and lowly.
And in this way we'll skip & play
On our road to Glory.

N. L.__ 1835 __ __ __

Henry DeWitt's

Come let us play and skip around

Henry DeWitt
New Lebanon, New York, 1835

Lively (♩=60)

Come let us play and skip a – round; Let us be in mo- tion; A

live in ev – 'ry gift be found In this pure de – vo – tion. We

sure – ly know it is the way To be meek and low – ly; And

in this way we'll skip and play On our road to Glor – y.

MS SV–A/**SU–2** pp. 72–73

O free – dom love – ly in my eyes To thee I'm bound in
du – ty In thee is an e – ter – nal prize Thy
ways are ways of beau – ty
As fawns up – on the
mount – ains height Or as the ea – gles in their flight To
be in per – fect lib – er – ty My soul does long to
be as free

Wrote by
Wm. C. Brackett
Watervliet Sept 6th 1835

Abram Perkins
Enfield N. H.

O freedom, lovely in my eyes

Abraham Perkins
Enfield, New Hampshire

Reverently (♩.=72)

O free- dom, love- ly in my eyes, To thee I'm bound in du - ty. In thee is an e- ter - nal prize; Thy ways are ways of beau - ty. Lo lo lo- dle lo lo lo, lo lo- dle lo lo lo, Lo lo lo- dle lo lo lo lo lo lo lo- dle lo lo lo. O lo lo. As fawns up- on the mount - ains height Or as the ea - gles in their flight, To be in per - fect lib - er- ty My soul does long to be as free. Lo lo lo- dle lo Lo lo. Lo lo lo- dle lo lo lo As lum lum.

MS SV–A/**SU–2** p. 76

O Lord do remember my soul
And hear me when I humbly pray
My thoughts words & action control
O guide me in thy holy way
All the rest of my life
While on earth I remain
How freely I spend it to thee
My souls salvation to gain

O Lord, do remember my soul

Abraham Perkins
North Enfield, New Hampshire

Gifts of the Spirit

MS SV-A/**SU-2** p. 78

O come good An - gels O make me spir- i- tual mind -

ed That I may feel the gifts of God for I do

hun - ger af - ter right - eous - ness. O

fill my soul O fill my soul with good things

Isaac N. Youngs
New Lebanon

Gifts of the Spirit

Isaac Youngs
New Lebanon, New York

Beseechingly (♩.=100)

O come good__ An – gels O make me spir- i - tual

mind– ed That I may feel the gifts of God for I___ do__

hun – ger af – ter_ right- eous – ness. O fill my__ soul

O fill__ my___ soul__ with good_ things.

MS SV–A/**SU–2** p. 83

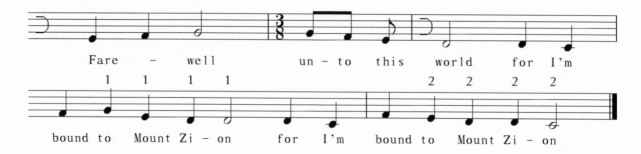

Fare – well un – to this world for I'm
1 1 1 1
bound to Mount Zi – on for I'm bound to Mount Zi – on
2 2 2 2

Father James'

Farewell unto this world

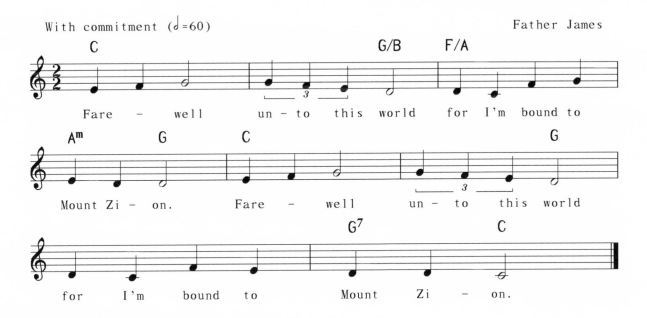

With commitment (♩=60)   Father James

Fare - well un - to this world for I'm bound to
Mount Zi - on. Fare - well un - to this world
for I'm bound to Mount Zi - on.

The Happiness of Being Good

MS SV–A/**SU-2** p. 84

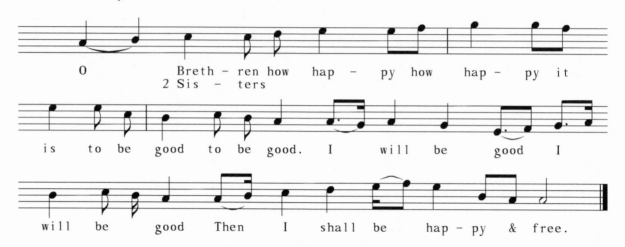

O   Breth – ren how   hap – py how   hap – py   it
    2 Sis – ters

is   to   be   good   to   be   good.   I   will   be   good   I

will   be   good   Then   I   shall   be   hap – py   &   free.

I. N. Youngs dream

The Happiness of Being Good

Joyfully (♩=120)

Isaac N. Youngs' dream

O_____ 1. Breth – ren how hap – py, how hap – py it
2. Sis – ters

is to be good, to be good. I___ will be good, I___

will be__ good; Then I shall be____ hap – py and free.

Little Big I

MS SV-A/**SU-2** p. 87

O little big I! I mean you shall die
I'll war I'll fight I'll make you fly.
How mean you are and how mean you shall fare
You've got to come down! down! flat to the ground.

North Enfield }
N. H. }

– 2 1 –

Little Big I

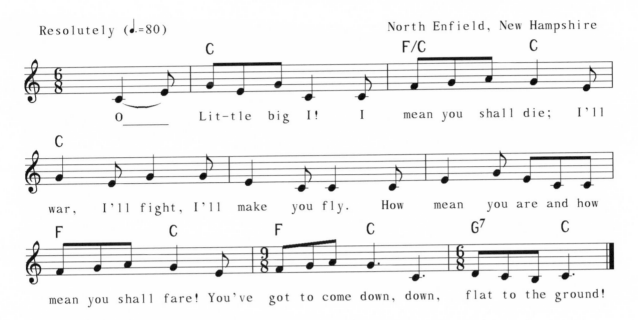

Resolutely (♩.=80)   North Enfield, New Hampshire

O _____ Lit-tle big I!   I   mean you shall die;   I'll

war,   I'll fight, I'll make   you fly.   How   mean   you are and how

mean you shall fare! You've got to come down, down,   flat to the ground!

Love and Peace

MS SV–A/**SU–2** p. 100

I want to feel love I want to feel peace
I want to have union in every feast
The love of the gospel the life of the soul
It brings consolation to both young & old.

–22–

Love and Peace

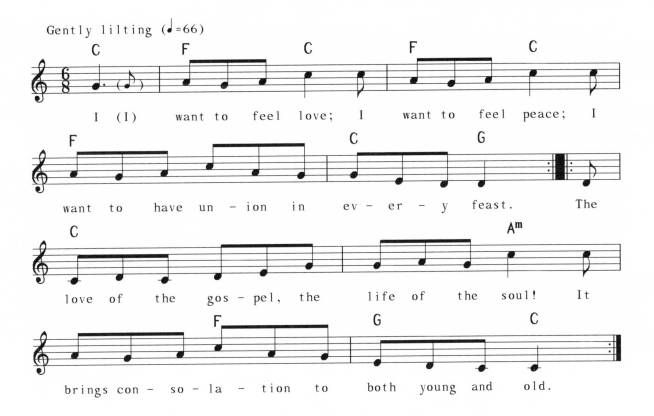

Gently lilting (♩=66)

I (I) want to feel love; I want to feel peace; I want to have un – ion in ev – er – y feast. The love of the gos – pel, the life of the soul! It brings con – so – la – tion to both young and old.

Happy Band

MS SV–A/**SU–2** p. 145

O see this lit – tle hap – py Band All

mov – ing on to Zi – ons land

While in their true de –

vo – tion Their hands & feet in mo – tion

New Lebanon ~~~~~

–23–

Happy Band

Sweet Communion

MS SV–A/**SU–2** p. 154

Now in love & un – ion Let us move a – long to – geth – er

In this sweet com – mun – ion To love and bless each oth – er

S. Union ~~~~
Round Dance

Sweet Communion

Round Dance
South Union, Kentucky

Gently swinging (♩.=80-88)

Now in love and un – ion, Let us move a –

long to – geth – er, In this sweet com – mun – ion, To

love and bless each oth – er. Lo – dle lo – dle

lo – dle lo lo – dle lo – dle lo – dle lo lo

lo – dle lo – dle lo – dle lo lo – dle lo – dle lo – dle lum lum.

Round Dance

MS SV–A/**SU–2** p. 163

There's   noth – ing on   the   earth to   bind us

While with   saints we   are   u – nit – ing   Lo   we   leave the
                                                                1   2

world be– hind us; An – gels   are   in   –   vit – ing.

H. L. Eades.
S. Union

Round Dance

H. L. Eades
South Union, Kentucky

With joyous assurance (♩.=96)

There's_ noth - ing on the earth to bind_ us
While, with saints, we are u - nit - ing. Lo, we leave the
world be- hind us; An - gels are in - vit - ing. There's
vit - ing. Lo lo lo lo lo lo lo lo
lo lo lo- dle lo lo- dle lo lo- dle lo, Lo lo lo lo
lo- dle lo lo lo lo lo lo lo lum lum.

MS SV–A/**SU–2** p. 179

Shout shout   shout & sing,   shout & make the   Heav– ens ring,

Shout   & praise the   God   a – bove   While   An – gels cloth us

with   his love.

Southunion
Jan. 2, 1848.

Shout, shout, shout and sing

South Union, Kentucky
January 2, 1848

With gusto (♩=116)

Shout, shout, shout and sing, Shout and make the

Heav – ens ring! Shout and praise the God a – bove, While

An – gels clothe us with his love. Lo – rel lo lo- rel

lo lo – rel lo – rel lo lo- rel lo – rel lo

lo- rel lo lo- rel lo lo lo lo- rel lo- rel lo lo lo.

MS SV–A/**SU–2** p. 182

Shout shout ye lit- tle child- ren Shout shout shout & sing.

Shout shout & clap your hands And praise your ho - ly

Sav - ior Moth - er.

S. Union

Shout, shout, ye little children

With animation (♩=112–120)

South Union, Kentucky

MS SV−A/**SU−2** p. 218

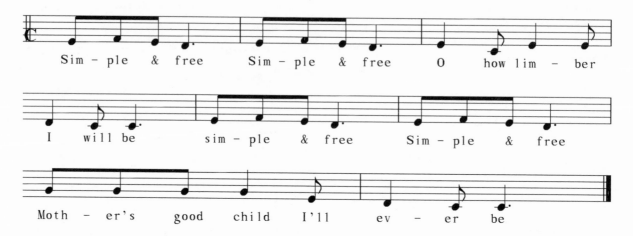

Sim − ple & free Sim − ple & free O how lim − ber

I will be sim − ple & free Sim − ple & free

Moth − er's good child I'll ev − er be

S Union

Simple and free

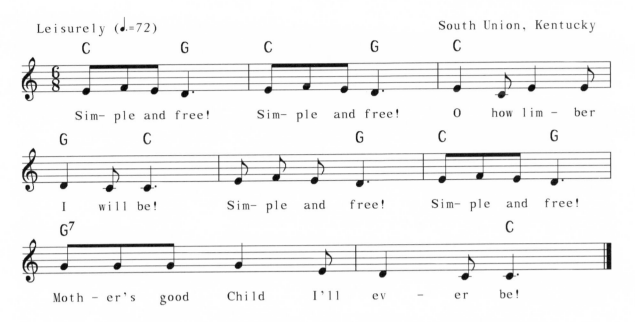

Leisurely (♩.=72)

South Union, Kentucky

Sim- ple and free! Sim- ple and free! O how lim – ber

I will be! Sim- ple and free! Sim- ple and free!

Moth – er's good Child I'll ev – er be!

Heavenly Stream

MS SV–A/**SU–2** p. 220

O here is the stream the pure liv-ing stream The
stream of heav-en-ly wa – ters O come & drink &
be re – fresh'd All Moth – ers Sons & Daugh – ters

South Union

Heavenly Stream

With sweet assurance (♩.=76)   South Union, Kentucky

O here is the stream, the pure liv – ing stream, The

stream of heav-en – ly wa – ters; O come and drink and

be__ re – fresh'd, All Moth – ers Sons_ and Daugh – ters.

Lo lo – dle lo – dle lo – dle lo lo, Lo

lo – dle lo- dle lo lum lum, Lo lo- dle lo lo lo

lo- dle lo lo, Lo lo – dle lo – dle lum._____

A Laughing Song

MS SV–A/**SU-2** pp. 225–226

Why I won- der you dont laugh a lit- tle laugh a lit- tle &

laught a lit – tle Why I won- der you aint all reel – ing

back – wards for – wards side – wards and down – wards

Why I won- der you can go so straight & keep such a slick &

cu – ri- ous shape For of Moth- ers wine I've got a small por- tion It

sets me in – to a stag – ger- ing mo – tion Well well I'm

will- ing to stag- ger stag – ger stag – ger a – way from bond – age

Well well I'm will- ing to reel reel reel reel in- to free- dom.

A Laughing Song

MS SV–A/**SU-2** P. 231

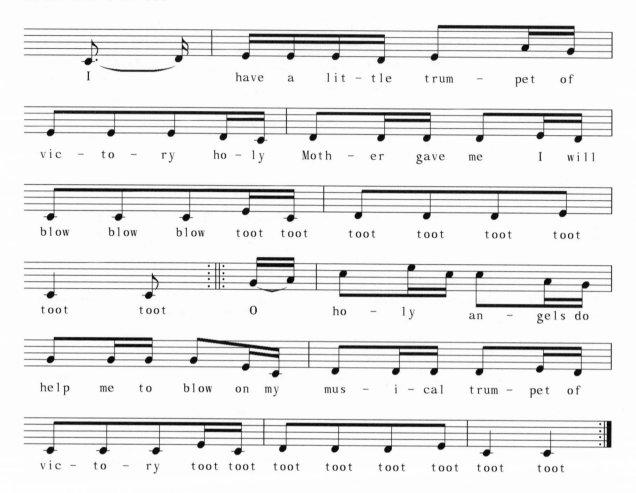

I have a lit – tle trum – pet of vic – to – ry ho – ly Moth – er gave me I will blow blow blow toot toot toot toot toot toot toot toot O ho – ly an – gels do help me to blow on my mus – i – cal trum – pet of vic – to – ry toot toot toot toot toot toot toot toot

South Union
recopied Feb. 4 1849

I have a little trumpet

South Union, Kentucky
Recopied February 4, 1849

MS SV–A/**SU–2** p. 232

S Union

Drink ye of Mother's wine

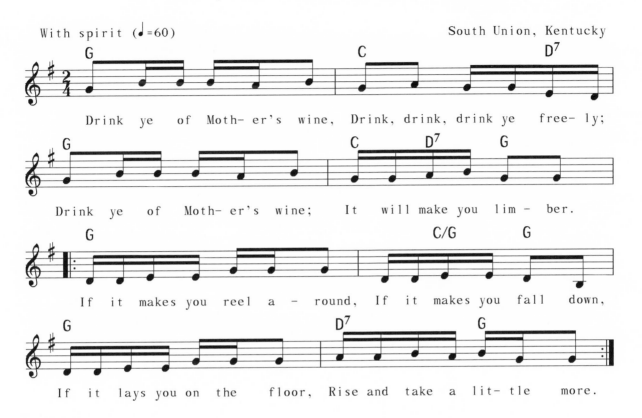

With spirit (♩=60)   South Union, Kentucky

Drink ye of Moth- er's wine, Drink, drink, drink ye free- ly;

Drink ye of Moth- er's wine; It will make you lim - ber.

If it makes you reel a - round, If it makes you fall down,

If it lays you on the floor, Rise and take a lit- tle more.

MS SV-A/**SU-2** pp. 244-245

Lit- tle child- ren dont you want A pret- ty cup of Moth- er's wine

If you do on the floor's A cups thats worth pos - ses - sing

O it will your ves- sels fill With ho - ly pow- er life & zeal

If you bow bend or real You'll feel a lit - tle bet - ter

Pleasant Hill

Little children

¹Written as "cups" in the manuscript.

– 3 4 –

MS SV-A/**SU-2** p. 256

H. G.
South Union

72 | **Manuscript A**

Like a little busy bee

H. G.
South Union, Kentucky

Whimsically (♩=112)

Like a lit – tle bus – y bee, I'll fly a – round and gath – er hon – ey From ev – ery pret – ty flow'r, Which grows in Zi – on's bow – er. Come, ev – 'ry bus – y bee, Ye may free – ly share with me; O it is a pret – ty trea– sure From our ho – ly_____ Moth – er.

2

Manuscript B

"A Communication from the Saviour"

This manuscript, entitled "A Communication from the Saviour to the Holy Anointed and Elders, for the Inhabitants of Zion. Holy Mount, Oct. 1, 1845," appears to be a record of gifts received through spiritual manifestation at Holy Mount (the spiritual and also feast site name for New Lebanon) during just one day of the period of spiritual manifestation that stretched from 1837 to 1847. Younger members, in particular, both stimulated and were stimulated by an outpouring of spiritual visitations, invisible gifts, gift songs, and other such phenomena. Because so many Shakers experienced trances in which they saw the spirit of Mother Ann Lee speaking to them, dancing with them, and giving them an outpouring of gift songs, this period of spiritual manifestation is referred to as Mother's Work or Mother Ann's Work.

Spiritual manifestations, first showing up in Kentucky, began early in the Shaker experience, but the manifestations of spiritual revival that occurred between 1837 and 1847 produced an outpouring of thousands of songs, including those received at Holy Mount. This decade of spiritual manifestation began when very young girls at Watervliet, New York, fell into trances, reported seeing angels and heavenly sights, and exhibited unusual bodily movements. Within a few months of hearing news of these manifestations, other Shaker communities began to experience visitations and strenuous dancing inspired by "religious highs," along with the spirit-gift songs already mentioned.

The youthfulness of many of the recipients who were the "instruments" of spiritual visitations and gifts, and in particular, the gift songs, furnished an interesting contrast to the long-established musical primacy of the older Shakers. A significant number of these people had a respected amount of musical training and had contributed most of the earlier "solemn songs" (songs without text), hymns, anthems, and dance tunes. Though this older group of musicians still contributed songs, songmaking now became more democratized, as hundreds of trance-induced songs poured forth from the great body of Shakers, among whom were so many of the young.

This manuscript contains two letters, signed "The Savior" rather than "Saviour" (the latter spelling appearing in the title of the manuscript), and only two songs, the hymns "The Saviour's Universal Prayer" and "And again, O Heavenly Father." There are also seventy-three Bible-style revelations, followed by the notation "Joel Chap III 28–32." Revelation 66 asks the Elders to "let the people of each society tho'out Zion, on the 25th day of December at 9 o'clock A.M. assemble themselves in one body and in one spirit, in their place of sacred worship, and sing the—*Saviour's Universal Prayer* sent forth by mine own hand." A note appended to the seventy-three revelations advises "that there should be as accurate a record of the proceedings of this day written, as can consistently be done, by each individual Society . . . there should be a record of this day sent from each society to the ministry at Holy Mount." Following this note is another communication: "It is my desire that all who have had any manifestation of, or relative to, the present gift should communicate it to their Elders . . . Amen. *The Savior*." The spiritual gifts on this occasion seem to have been the seventy-three revelations and the two hymns.

David R. Lamson, in his 1848 eyewitness account *Two*

Fig. 5. Interior of the Meeting Room in the First Meetinghouse (1786–1938) at Hancock, Massachusetts. WILLIAM F. WINTER JR., "INTERIOR OF MEETING ROOM," 1931, PHOTOGRAPH FROM HABS, LIBRARY OF CONGRESS.

Fig. 6. The Meetinghouse, Hancock, Massachusetts. The building was moved in 1962 from the Shirley site (1793–1908). Separate entrances as seen here are enduring examples of the Shaker practice of separating men and women. This separation included non-Shaker visitors who attended meetinghouse services. COURTESY JAMES D. OPDAHL.

Fig. 7. Woodcut: Hancock Mountain Meeting. REPRINTED FROM DAVID R. LAMSON, *Two Years' Experience among the Shakers*, 1848, FRONTISPIECE.

Years Experience Among the Shakers, introduced his description of the mountain meetings with reference to revelations at New Lebanon. He "drew a word picture" detailing the layout of the Hancock feast site where the sacred ceremony he witnessed while living with the Hancock Shakers occurred:

> About the year 1841, or—42, a very important revelation was received at (New Lebanon) requiring every society . . . to prepare a place upon some mountain, or hill, in its vicinity, for a Holy place of worship. The place pointed out for our society was about a mile and a half from our village . . . It is in sight of the mountain chosen for their meeting ground, by the society at New Lebanon, called Mt. Lebanon. . . . The brethrens went to work . . . and prepare . . . the ground. . . . Near the centre is a little spot, enclosed with a fence . . . in form a hexagon. It is called "the Fountain."[1]

Lamson further wrote that a marble slab, engraved with the purpose, date, and Lord's instructions for creating such a place, was set up at the northern end of the cleared site within a fenced-in area called the spiritual fountain. A fence of a large perimeter enclosed the entire site, including the smaller fenced-in fountain area (fig. 7). Lamson observed that during the ceremony the Shakers wore invisible overlays of spiritual clothing atop their Shaker garments, drank invisible wine, ate invisible food, and received invisible gifts.[2]

The spiritual nature of the mountain experiences in the various communities transported many of the Shakers into a "religious high," intensified by prophetic exhortations, exuberant singing, and spirited dancing. Shakers believed that famous people, members who had died, biblical figures, and Mother Ann Lee herself visited them in spirit form at these ceremonies. Lamson reported that Shakers believed that these spirits entered entranced Shakers and used them as "instruments" through which they, the spirits, talked, danced, and bestowed gifts of song and prophecy.[3]

This intense religious fervor cooled by the middle of the nineteenth century. When the feast site at Mount Lebanon was vandalized in 1846, one year after the date of this manuscript, the Shakers allowed it to fall into disuse. The feast ground rites in community after community began to give way to more structured and less promiscuous expressions of dancing and singing. The Shakers at New Lebanon and in the other communities still used their meetinghouses for regular worship ceremonies, however, just as they had done before and during the height of the era of spiritual manifestation (see figs. 5 and 6).

The revival movement that had also penetrated grassroot religious segments of the American public waned as well. America was increasingly reaching out for the material benefits of growing industrialization and the attendant rise of secular leisure activities. As a consequence, the Shakers began to experience a decline in the demand for their meticulously crafted products and a resultant drop in income. At the same time, the communal religious life offered by the Shakers failed to attract working-age converts as it had once done. Finally, as existing members aged, they could not maintain the highly energetic movements once exercised in Shaker worship, song, and dance.

The Saviour's Universal Prayer

MS SV–B/NL pp. 33–34

Our fa – ther, who art in Heaven hal – lowed be Thy name, Thy king – dom come, Thy will be done on earth as it is done in Heav– en. Give us this day our dai – ly bread, and for – give us our debts as we for – give our debt – ors. Leave us not in temp – ta – tion but de – liv– er us from e – vil, for Thine is the king – dom, the glo – ry and pow– er for– ev– er more A – men.

The Saviour's Universal Prayer

Slowly and reverently

MS SV-B/NL pp. 34–36

4

And a - gain, O Heav- en - ly Fa - ther

Hear thy child - rens hum - ble cry,

For o'er earth thy wing doth hov - er

Bear - ing judg - ments from on high

While thy jus - tice strews thy judg - ments

Lo, thy mer - cy cries re - pent

Help thy child - ren heed thy warn - ings

By the Proph - ets thou hast sent.

2. Open eyes that now are blinded,
    Unstop ears that now are deaf,
    Check the heady and high minded,
    To the sufferers give relief,
    Melt the heart that now is hearken
    Loose the tongue that now is bound,
    To the humble seeker hearken,
    Let repentance flow around.

3. Bind the tongue that does not praise thee
    Clothe the froward soul with fear
    Blow the trump and wake thy children
    Call the nations far and near,
    Fill the weak with holy power
    Clothe the pure and bless the meek
    Let repentance like a shower
    Cause all souls thy way to seek

4. Bear a light to those unshrouded
    In the shades of sinful night,
    Let the days of grace be cloudless,
    That all nations see thy light.
    Hear, O hear, Almighty Father,
    Those who seek in humble prayer
    All who lean upon thy power.
    Make the objects of thy care.

And again, O Heavenly Father

Slowly and reverently

1. And a - gain, O Heav - en - ly Fa - ther,
2. O - pen eyes that now___ are blind - ed,
3. Bind the tongue that does___ not praise thee,
4. Bear a light to those___ un - shroud - ed

Hear thy child - ren's hum - ble cry,
Un - stop ears that now are deaf,
Clothe the fro - ward soul with fear,
In___ the shades of sin - ful night;

For o'er earth thy wing___ doth hov - er
Check the head - y and high - mind - ed,
Blow thy trump and wake___ thy___ child - ren,
Let thy day of grace___ be___ cloud - less

Bear - ing judg - ments from on high.
To the - suf - f'rers give re - lief,
Call___ the na - tions far and near,
That___ all na - tions see thy light.

While thy jus - tice strews thy judg - ments,
Melt the heart that now___ is hard - ened,
Fill the weak with ho - ly pow - er,
Hear, O hear, Al - might - y Fa - ther,

Lo,___ thy mer - cy cries___ re - pent;
Loose___ the tongue that now___ is bound,
Clothe___ the pure and bless___ the meek,
Those___ who seek in hum___ ble - pray'r

Help thy child - ren heed thy___ warn - ings
To the hum - ble seek - er, har - ken,
Let re - pen - tance like a show - er
All who lean up - on thy___ pow - er,

By the Proph - ets thou___ hast sent.
Let re - pent - ance flow___ a - round.
Cause all souls___ thy way___ to seek.
Make the ob - jects of___ thy care.

3

Manuscript C

"Behold I Come Quickly and My Promise Is Sure"

There are no staffs in any of the songs in this manuscript, but there seems to have been a very conscientious attempt to keep notes and text coordinated, to bar all measures, and to include modal symbols. The earlier entries are entered in small compact print, the later ones in a larger and freer print, but the formation of the uppercase letters, as well as that of lowercase letters, in the two types of entries seems very consistent. Was there one scribe or two entering songs? Even if the scribe or scribes were identified, unless a diary, journal, or letter exists to allow for a handwriting comparison, it could be risky to draw conclusions. Patterson, certainly, refrained from using penmanship as proof of authorship of songs. He wrote, "The penmanship of a large group of girls writing at Lebanon in the late 1830s and 1840s, for example, was astonishingly uniform, and I do not attempt to play my hunches."[1]

Dates found on songs in this manuscript range from 1849 to 1903. Here, again, is a problem for the researcher: does the date indicate when a Shaker composed, or recorded, or received the song? Is it in fact all three? Or is it some other possibility altogether? In terms of site source identification, "New Lebanon" appears more often than does any other community, but what does this imply? As Cook observes, "The free exchange of music between communities, and the anonymity of many of the copyists, add to the confusion of dating the hymnals or locating them by community." Other causes for confusion that he touches upon are the writing down of songs years after their having been first heard or sung, the movement of hymnals from one community to another as communities closed, and the predilections of individual scribes.[2]

Hearing the handful of Shakers at Hancock sing "Who will bow and bend like a willow" gave us our first introduction to the very abrupt endings often used as part of the Shaker singing style. In 1997, Roger Hall, having finished tabulating the frequency with which Shaker songs have been electronically recorded, reported that this song ranked third in popularity.[3] First and second were "Simple Gifts" and "Come Life, Shaker Life." Brother Ricardo's detailed instructions for performing a Shaker dance to accompany "Who will bow" may be found in section 10 of this book.

Songs that appear to be nonsense, and dialect songs in foreign, Native American, or African American tongues, are scattered throughout Shaker song manuscript books. Many of them came to the Shakers as gift songs they received from spirits when in a trance or by way of a dream.

Shakers were not reluctant to compose or to spiritually receive gift songs containing nonsense syllables. In this manuscript, "March" begins with the syllables "ve vo vive vana" but then flows into a blessing from Mother Ann Lee: "I will walk with you says your blessed Mother Ann and I will comfort you my little band."

Two dialect songs appear on the same page in this manuscript. A Shaker, perhaps in a trance or a dream, verbalized the text of "In de shiny Muder's mansion" in a Native American or slave dialect. As a point of interest, visits by Native American spirits to feast grounds, meetinghouses, and other spiritual sites were common phenomena, particularly during the 1835–1847 period of spiritual manifestation.

Andrews wrote that "Bonny Wee One," the second dialect song, came from Holy Ground, the spiritual name for the Canterbury, New Hampshire, community.[4] The text is in a

Scottish dialect that, in the case of some words, gives the impression of having suffered from too long a separation from Scotland and its translation has been challenging.

Seven of the dialect words in the song have posed little or no difficulty. There is common agreement among many sources on the translations of *Mither, gude, toche, frae, hae, mickle,* and *ye,* but not so for such words as *la, le, fane, fende (feude, fude, faynd),* and *tether (tither).* The existence of the spelling variations that appear in manuscript and in published copies of the song, as well as the dearth of hyphens in general, poses a challenge to the translator. Sources of the difficulty could well be misspellings by the Shaker scribes because of a lack of familiarity with Scottish dialect. Perhaps the Shaker who received the song at Holy Ground did not enunciate with sufficient clarity. There is also the possibility that the Shaker, so possessed, was too far removed from his or her Scottish background to have had adequate understanding of or proficiency in Scottish dialect.

Some spellings have no translatable meanings; others have meanings, but they are out of context and make no sense. Our consultants on Scottish dialect were quick to recognize that both the misspelling and the corruption of Scottish words in the song serve as barriers to smooth and accurate translations. In spite of these difficulties, we venture to offer two rather incomplete translations gathered from the several sources we consulted. Knowing that Shakers experienced spirit visitations from their gift-giving founder, Mother Ann Lee, we can, with some certainty, believe that this is a gift song and that the mother in the song is the spirit of Mother Ann Lee. Two partial and very tentative translations follow:

I'm a Scotch bonny wee one	I'm a Scotch bonny wee one
My Mother so good	My Mother so good
Has sent ___?___	Has sent you in good faith (?)
Some so happily and ___?___	Some say fine and tempting (?)
'Tis a dowry (?) And another (?)	'Tis a dowry (?) and a marriage (?)
From the bonny highland heather	From the bonny highland heather
Will you have it? Will you have it?	Will you have it? Will you have it?
It will do you much good.	It will do you much good.

MS SV–C/XU–**2** p. 6

Shake & shuf – fle out of pride Shake While sin and

death a – bide Shake and shuf – fle out of e – vil

Shake shake sub – due the Dev – il

New Lebanon. N. Y.

Shake and shuffle out of pride

With spirit (♩.=120)   New Lebanon, New York

Shake   and   shuf – fle   out   of   pride;

Shake   While   sin   and   death   a – bide;

Shake   and   shuf – fle   out   of   e – vil;

Shake,   shake, sub – due   the Dev – il.   Lo   lo lo – rel

lo   lo   lo – rel,   Lo   lo – rel   lo   lo   lo – rel

Lo   lo lo – rel   lo   lo   lo – rel,   Lo   lo – rel   lum   lum.

MS SV–C/XU–2 p. 8

(Lodle lo lodle lodle lodle lo)

Sweet Union

MS SV–C/XU–2 p. 9

Sweet un – ion and peace faith – ful souls can en –

joy There's noth – ing on earth can such un – ion des –

troy The ho ho ho Moth– er says they shall

be As a beau – ti – ful Star'n E – ter– ni – ty

Sweet Union

With resolve (♩=100)

Sweet__ un – ion and peace faith-ful souls can en –

joy; There's noth – ing on earth can such un – ion des –

troy. The ho, ho, ho, Moth – er says they shall

be As a beau – ti- ful Star in E – ter – ni – ty.

Round Dance

MS SV–C/XU–2 p. 12

Now be lim – ber as a with Bend and bow in

mo – tion Nev – er fear to turn or twist

In this pure de – vo – tion Have no bond – age

in the ease Free- dom sure is bet – ter Those who run the

gos – pel race, must shake off ev – ery fet – ter

— 40 —

Round Dance

Lilting (♩.=106)

Now be lim – ber as a withe; Bend and bow in

mo – tion. Nev – er fear to turn or twist

In this pure de – vo – tion. Have no bond – age

in the ease. Free- dom sure is bet – ter. Those who run the

gos – pel race must shake off ev – 'ry fet – ter.

Little Dove

MS SV–C/**XU**–**2** p. 13

I am a lit–tle dove from the heaven–ly world a – bove

I was brought un – to you by the An – gel of love

He brought me on his wings from the ho – ly Se – lan

A rich pres– ent un – to you from your good Moth– er Ann

Harvard

Little Dove

Sweetly (♩=60)   Harvard, Massachusetts

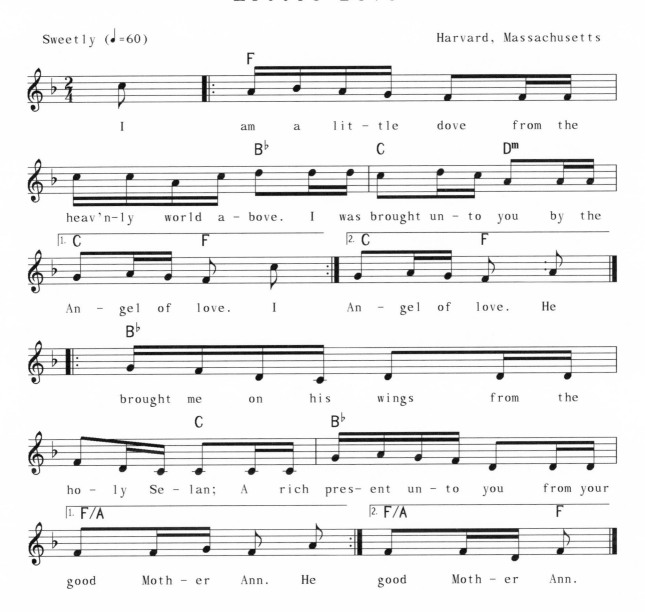

I am a lit-tle dove from the heav'n-ly world a-bove. I was brought un-to you by the An-gel of love. I An-gel of love. He brought me on his wings from the ho-ly Se-lan; A rich pres-ent un-to you from your good Moth-er Ann. He good Moth-er Ann.

Hear Mother Calling

MS SV-C/XU-2 p. 15

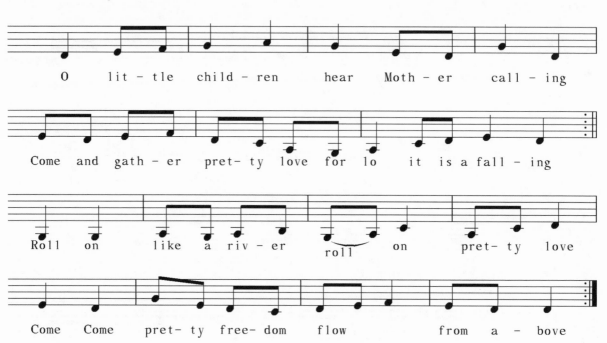

O lit – tle child – ren hear Moth – er call – ing

Come and gath – er pret – ty love for lo it is a fall – ing

Roll on like a riv – er roll on pret – ty love

Come Come pret – ty free-dom flow from a – bove

Hear Mother Calling

MS SV–C/XU–2 p. 19

I'll bow and I'll bend I'll stag – ger I'll reel

I'll twist and I'll turn If Moth– er's love I can feel

I'll skip and I'll play I'll shake from bond– age free

I'll bow and I'll bend

MS SV–C/XU–2 p. 20

Little children, gather love

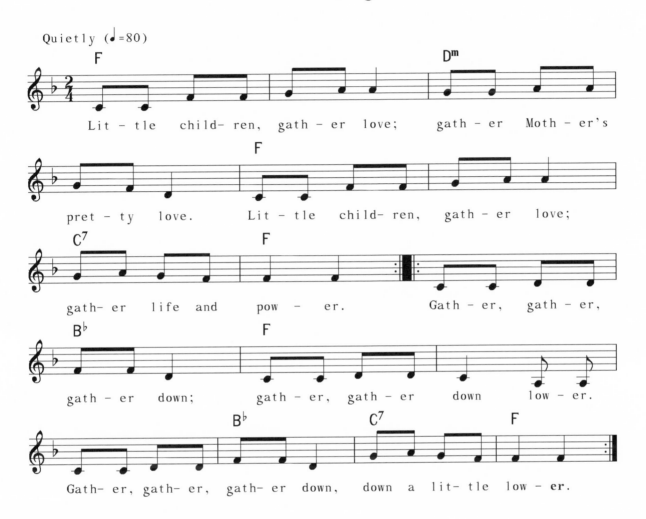

March

MS SV–C/**XU–2** p. 23

Ve   vo   vi – ve va–na vi   vo   vi – ve vum   Vi

vo   vi – ve   va – na   vo   vum   vum   vum   I

will   bless   the   ho– ly   I   will   bless   the   low– ly   I   will

bless   the   soul   who   will   for – ward   go   I   will

walk   with   you   says your   bless– ed   Moth– er   Ann   I   will

com – fort you   my   lit – tle   band   If   you   will   faith – ful

faith – ful   stand   I will   lead   you   safe – ly   by   the   hand.

March

(♩=66–72)

Ve__ vo vi- ve va- na vi__ vo vi- ve vum Vi__

vo vi- ve va - na vo vum vum vum. "I will

bless the ho- ly; I will bless the__ low- ly; I will

bless the soul who will for - ward go. I will

walk with you," says your bless- ed Moth- er Ann. "I will

com - fort you, my__ lit - tle band. If__ you will faith- ful,

faith- ful__ stand, I will lead you safe - ly by the hand."

Bonny Wee One

MS SV-C/XU-2 p. 28

I'm a Scotch bon- ny we one My

Mith- er soe gude Has sent ye la le some Sa

fane and feude 'Tis a toche and a teth- er Frae the

bon- ny high- land heath- er Will ye hae it will ye hae It It will

do ye mic – kle gude

Bonny Wee One

MS SV-C/XU-2 p. 28

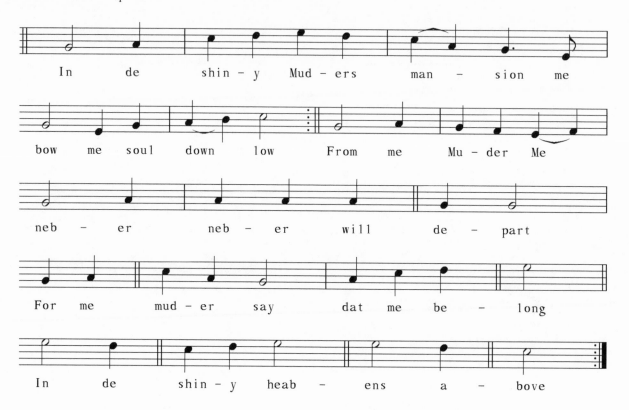

In de shin - y Mud - ers man - sion me

bow me soul down low From me Mu - der Me

neb - er neb - er will de - part

For me mud - er say dat me be - long

In de shin - y heab - ens a - bove

In de shiny Muder's mansion

Freely, like a chant (♩=138)

In de shin - y Mud - er's man - sion me

bow me soul down__ low. From me Mud - er Me___

neb - er, neb- er will de - part For me Mud - er say

dat me be - long In de shin - y heab- ens a - bove.

MS SV-C/**XU-2** p. 29

Who will bow and bend like a willow

MS SV–C/**XU–2** p. 53

I feel the gen – tle bree – zes blow From
Zi – ons ho – ly Moun – tain I see the Crys – tal
Wa – ters flow Down from the liv – ing Foun – tain
I see the doves the spot – less Doves That
hov – er all a – round us I see the Cord the
Gold – en Cord With which our Moth – er bound us

Given by Sarah Mason colored sister on the evening of her decease.
Harvard Mass.

I feel the gentle breezes blow

Sarah Mason
Harvard, Massachusetts

Gently flowing (♩=72)

I feel the gen – tle bree – zes blow From
Zi – on's ho – ly Moun – tain. I see the Crys – tal
Wa – ters flow Down from the liv – ing Foun – tain. I
see the doves, the spot – less Doves, That
hov – er all a – round us; I see the Cord, the
Gold – en Cord With which our Moth – er bound us.

MS SV-C/XU-2 pp. 66-67

Let the peo – ple be glad & my cho – sen re –
joice For lo the time has come When
thou – sands shall hear the glad sound of my
voice And Is – rael be gath – ered home I have
called to the North I have stretched to the
South my arm that is a – ble to Save I have
looked on the East I have breathed on the
West And I've walked on the Storm – y Wave.

Let the people be glad

MS SV–C/XU–*2* p. 81

Earth– ly pleas– ures I will leave

All her tur – moil & her grief

I'm travl – ing on – ward

to my home

In the man– sions of pure love

Mount Lebanon.

Earthly pleasures I will leave

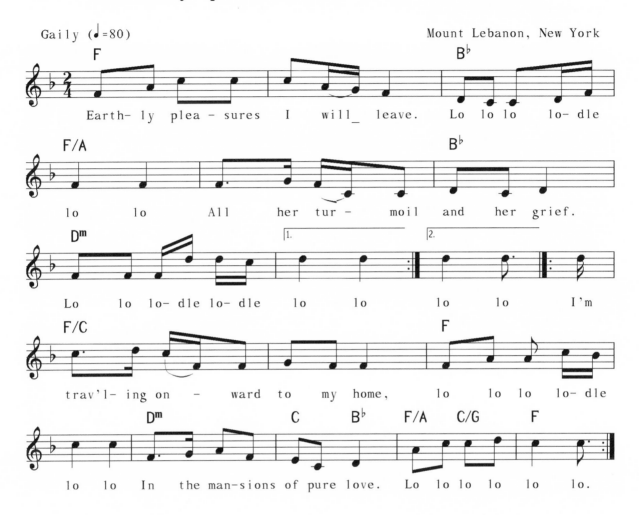

Gaily (♩=80)

Mount Lebanon, New York

Earth- ly plea - sures I will_ leave. Lo lo lo lo- dle

lo lo All her tur - moil and her grief.

Lo lo lo- dle lo- dle lo lo lo lo I'm

trav'l- ing on — ward to my home, lo lo lo lo- dle

lo lo In the man-sions of pure love. Lo lo lo lo lo lo.

MS SV-C/**XU-2** p. 89

We are all com–ing home We are all com–ing home We are all com–ing home home to our Par – ents Here our Fa – thers & our Moth – ers Here our Sis– ters & our Broth– ers Here our hous– es and our lands And here is life E – ter – nal

Eldress Mary Whicher

We are all coming home

Lyrically (♩=92)

Eldress Whicher

We are all com-ing home; We are all com-ing home; We are all com-ing home, home to our Par-ents. ents. Here our Fa-thers and our Moth-ers; Here our Sis-ters and our Broth-ers; Here our hous-es and our lands; And__ here is life E-ter-nal.

Bright Harpers

MS SV-C/**XU-2** pp. 106−107

Play on your harps your bright harps ye
bright harp-ers Sing ye song-sters of Je-ru-sa-lem
Strike on the notes so me-lo-di-ous and sweet
Sing sing Gods prais-es re-peat

Bright Harpers

Play on your harps, your bright harps, ye
bright harp - ers; Sing, ye___ song - sters
of Je - ru - sa - lem. Strike on the notes so me -
lo - di - ous and sweet; Sing, sing God's prais - es re - peat.
Lo lo - dle lo lo - dle lo - dle lo - dle lo,
Lo lo - dle lo lo - dle lo - dle lo - dle lum.
Lo lo - dle lo lo - dle lo - dle lo - dle lo
lo lo - dle lo lo - dle lo - dle lo - dle lum.

Sweet Afton

MS SV–C/XU–2 pp. 118–119

The An – gels have come to the dark sad – dened

earth Where wear – y & tear – ful the poor Pil – grims

sigh They bring the sweet pleas – ures Whose ra – di – ant

birth Is found in the man – sions of Glo – ry on high.

O sweet is the fountain of deep dwelling life
And clear are the waters which flow from above
While bless'd are the visons where warring & strife
Are lost in the brightness of heavenly love.
The voices of angels resounding in dome
Thro' whose silent regions the low wispers roll
And accents of peace from heavens bright home
Returned to that depths of the echoing soul.
Now rolls the deep darkness of error away
And sad weeping mourners are joyfully blessed
While opens the dawn of the bright beaming day
Which brings to each bosom its promise of rest.

Sweet Afton

4

Manuscript D

"I Feel a Sweet Influence upon Us"

Cook included this manuscript in his collation list of Shaker manuscripts.[1] It is the only manuscript for which he named the Hancock Shaker community as the provenance. This drew our attention, because the manuscript—one of the nine that we own—came to us by way of Jerry and Sybil Count from Brother Ricardo Belden, who had lived since 1917 in the Hancock Shaker community. We would like to establish that this manuscript originated at Hancock but, unfortunately, the above knowledge is too limited to provide absolute proof that it did so.

Not all songs in this manuscript have dates affixed to them. Those songs that are dated range from 1882 to 1903 in the first two thirds of the manuscript and from 1850 into the 1870s in the last third. Only one song has an earlier date: 1849. As we discussed in the preface and in the introduction to Manuscript C, dates affixed to songs in the manuscripts are open to a variety of interpretations.

As in the previous manuscript, the songs in this one are mainly quick songs with an occasional hymn. The songs have no staffs or bars, and only one song in the collection bears a title. Although all of the songs appear in small letteral notation, the noticeably varied handwriting speaks to more than one scribe making entries. None of the other manuscripts in our collection have as many obsolete or archaic variants, and misspellings, as this one does; they appear in eight of the fifteen songs included here and include *sercher* for searcher, *brethern* for breth'ren, *togeather* for together, *alway* for always, *relmes* for realms, and *valiently* for valiantly. The scribe also used *to* rather than *too* in "O what will the harvest be" and *invites* rather than *invite* in "I seek not the world."

The writing on some songs is freeflowing, and beams more than two notes long wave like banners above or below the notes. Bar lines denote measures, text and notes line up, and modal symbols exist. There are no staffs. The many music manuscript aids make for easy transcription of songs here.

Among the songs we selected from this manuscript is the well-known "'Tis the gift to be simple," or "Simple Gifts" (see fig. 8). Aaron Copland composed variations on this tune for his ballet suite "Appalachian Spring" in 1943–1944 and, in 1945, arranged the composition for use by symphony orchestras.[2] Nearly twenty years later in Britain, Sydney Carter adapted the tune for his ballad-like "Lord of the Dance."[3] "Simple Gifts" is repeated in section ten, augmented with stories, dance instructions, and explanations of vocalization.

Tis the gift to be simple tis the gift to be free Tis the gift to come down where we ought to be And when we find our selves in the place just right Twill be in the valley of love and delight When true simplicity is gained To bow & to bend we shant be ashamed To turn turn will be our delight Till by turning turning we come around right

Fig. 8. "Simple Gifts." Small letteral notation (Manuscript D).

Fig. 9. Pastoral scene, Hancock, Massachusetts, in the early 1950s. Only a few Shakers, including Brother Ricardo Belden, were in residence at the time. AUTHORS' COLLECTION.

MS SV-D/X? p. 1

I feel a sweet in - fluence Up - on us de - scend- ing The

heav - ens and earth in pure un - ion is blend - ing The

An - gels are with us to - day O Far from my vi - sion the

dark clouds of sor - row Give hope & joy to

glad- den the Mor- row Ye An - gels who're with us to - day

Mount Lebanon

I feel a sweet influence

Gently assuring (♩.=69)

Mount Lebanon, New York

I feel a sweet in- flu- ence Up- on us de- scend- ing; The
heav- ens and earth in pure un - ion is blend- ing The
an - gels are with us to- day. O far from my vi - sion the
dark clouds of sor - row Give hope and joy to
glad - den the Mor - row, Ye An - gels who're with us to - day.

MS SV–D/X? p. 49

Trust in the Lord His will be done

Tho the temp – est rag – es & the storm comes down

He will guide our Barque O'er the bil – lows high

And land us safe – ly o – ver there by & by.

As a guide thro the dark his power has been

To the Serch – er for Truth he will lend a hand

A help – er to those who will help them – selves

And work for the spread of the Truth up – on earth

Harvard April 22, 1894
Andrew Barrett

Trust in the Lord

Andrew Barrett
Harvard, Massachusetts, April 22, 1894

MS SV–D/X? p. 59

Sow– ing the seed of the Spring – time Care– ful– ly let it

Fall Know– ing that la – ter Au – tumn Bring– eth a

har– vest to all If we have sown of ser – vice

To God & hu – man – i – ty Sure we shall

reap a har – vest Of Joy thro E – ter – ni – ty

Myra McLean of Harvard

Sowing the seed of the Springtime

Myra McLean
Harvard, Massachusetts

MS SV–D/X? p. 73

We're hap – py & free & no Powers that be Can

hind– er our Pro – gress to heav – en We're up – ward bound where

sin is not found Our lives un – to God are giv – en

So breth– ern & sis – ters we'll jour – ney a – long To

reach that heav– en of Glo – ry And when we are there in that

re – gion so fair We'll re – peat to the An – gels our stor – y

1898

Enfield __ North Family

We're happy and free

North Family
Enfield, 1898

MS SV-D/X? p. 79

Up with the An - gels on wings of light

Soar - ing to relms e - ter - nal - ly Bright

Noth - ing shall hind - er my souls de - light For

heav - en - ly bliss I would share O

come with me I will be your stay When

long seems the hour & dark the day

To - geath - er we'll sing Gods prais - es al - way In

man - sions so love - ly & Fair

Elder Clark __ Enfield

Up with the Angels

Elder Clark
Enfield, Connecticut

– 6 0 –

MS SV-D/X? p. 81

Andrew Barrett   Olive Branch

132 | **Manuscript D**

Come, come, the way is op'ning

Andrew Barrett
Olive Branch, Florida, 1902

March (♩=88-100)

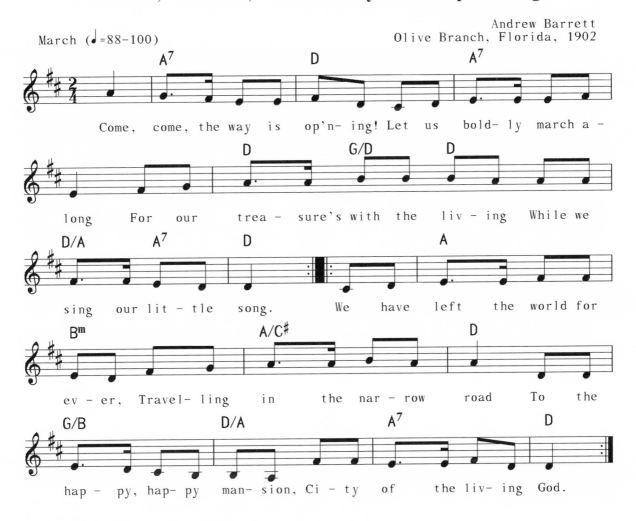

Come, come, the way is op'n- ing! Let us bold- ly march a-

long For our trea - sure's with the liv - ing While we

sing our lit - tle song. We have left the world for

ev - er, Travel- ling in the nar - row road To the

hap - py, hap- py man- sion, Ci - ty of the liv- ing God.

MS SV–D/X? p. 83

O what will the har- vest be, what will the

har- vest be What will the har- vest be When the grain is

cut When the wheat is gath- ered and bound in - to

sheaves And the har - vest - er gath - ers his

own When the thrash- ing work is thru And the

win- now – ing to O what will the har - vest be

Harvard   *Andrew Barrett*

O what will the harvest be

Andrew Barrett
Harvard, Massachusetts

MS SV-D/X? p. 109

I am loved as I love I am blest as I bless No
more or less will be giv – en to me The
mea– sure I meet will be mea – sured a – gain For
Just– ice is a law un – to all the same Then
let my ef – forts all be to love and bless And
strength– en the good in ev' – ry one Where –
ev – er I am called what ev – er I can do Shall be
spent in the cause of the good and true

Andrew Barrett   *Dec. 5th 1902*

I am loved as I love

Andrew Barrett
December 5th, 1902

Tranquilly (♩=96)

I am loved as I love; I am blest as I bless. No more or less will be giv – en to me. The mea- sure I meet will be mea – sured a – gain For___ Just– ice is a law un – to all the same. Then let my ef – forts all be to love and bless And strength – en the good in ev' – ry one. Where – ev – er I am called; what – ev – er I can do Shall be spent in the cause of the good and true.

MS SV–D/X? p. 118

We are strong in the Lord & his might For his
cause we're a val – ient Band The truth is our Cit- a – del of
strength Where con – quering arm – ies round us stand We are
strong we are strong In the
con – quest of right o – ver wrong In the
Bat – tle of life we will tri – umph And
shout we are strong we are strong

No darkness of doubt shall enshroud
Nor fear tho our foes assail
The truth is our everlasting choice
In its conquering power will prevail
We are strong.

We are strong in the Lord

MS SV–D/X? p. 119

Mt_Lebanon

With my own hand I will shake

With emphasis (♩=120–132)   Mount Lebanon, New York

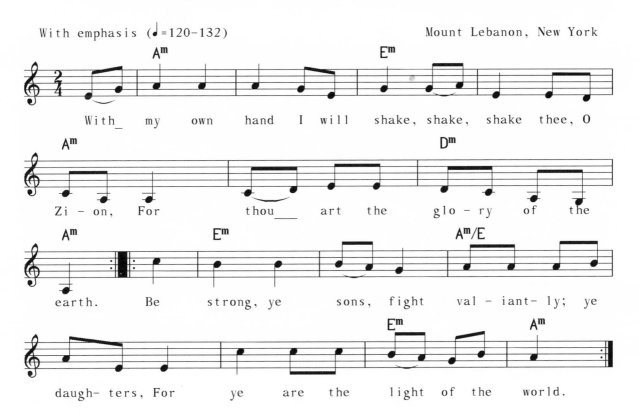

With my own hand I will shake, shake, shake thee, O
Zi – on, For thou art the glo – ry of the
earth. Be strong, ye sons, fight val – iant- ly; ye
daugh- ters, For ye are the light of the world.

MS SV–D/X? p. 132

Hark the mer – ry Bells are ring – ing While we

tar – ry here be – low Hear the lit – tle Bells are

ring– ing Ring – ing ring– ing ev – er more

They are call – ing us to – geath – er In – to

Un – ion & sweet Love Where to love & bless each

oth – er As the An – gels do a – bove

White Water

Hark! The merry Bells are ringing

MS SV–D/X? p. 154

I seek not the world or its plea – sures My
love to Gods peo– ple I hold Is worth more than all earth rich
trea – sures Her myr– iads of sil– ver and gold O
let noth – ing earth – ly di – vide us Or
cause our spir– its to roam Our fa – ther & Moth– er in –
vites us To heav – en that beau – ti – ful home

Eldress Betsy Smith
South Union Ky

— 66 —

I seek not the world

Eldress Betsy Smith
South Union, Kentucky

Calm anticipation (♩.=66-72)

seek not the world or its plea - sures; My love to God's peo - ple I hold; Is worth more than all earth's rich trea - sures, Her myr- iads of sil - ver and gold. O let noth - ing earth- ly di - vide us Or cause our____ spir - its to roam. Our fa - ther and moth - er in - vite us To heav - en, that beau - ti - ful home.

MS SV-D/X? p. 171

Tis the gift to be sim – ple tis the

gift to be free Tis the gift to come down

where we ought to be And when we find our selves in the

place just right Twill be in the val – ley of love and de –

light When true sim – plic– i– ty is gained To

bow & to bend we shant be a – shamed To turn turn will

be our de – light Till by turn– ing turn– ing we come around right

'Tis the gift to be simple

Quick dance (♩=120–130)

MS SV–D/X? p. 174

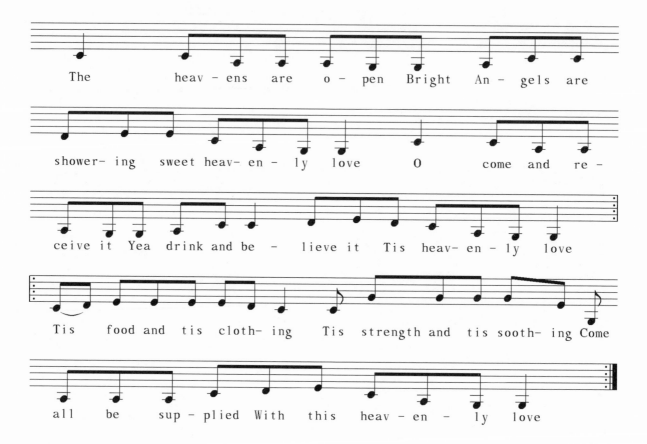

The heav – ens are o – pen Bright An – gels are
shower– ing sweet heav– en – ly love O come and re –
ceive it Yea drink and be – lieve it Tis heav– en – ly love
Tis food and tis cloth– ing Tis strength and tis sooth– ing Come
all be sup – plied With this heav – en – ly love

From Canterbury

The heavens are open

Tenderly (♩.=66)

Canterbury, New Hampshire

The heav- ens are o - pen; Bright An - gels are show- 'ring sweet

heav- en - ly love. O come and re - ceive it; Yea,

drink and be - lieve it; 'Tis heav- en - ly love. 'Tis

food and 'tis cloth- ing; 'Tis strength and 'tis sooth- ing; Come,

all be sup - plied With this heav- en - ly love.

MS SV–D/X? p. 178

Ive got a ver – y de – li – cious crumb Sweet – er
far than hon – ey If you want Ill give you
some It cant be bought with mon – ey
Bless – ed Moth – er gave it me Ho – ly
ho – ly love love Pure and good as good can
be Right from heav – en a – bove

Sent to Andrew Barrett

Mt Lebanon
1855

I've got a very delicious crumb

Sent to Andrew Barrett
Mount Lebanon, New York, 1855

With delight (♩.=100)

I've got a ver-y de-li-cious crumb;
Sweet-er far__ than hon-ey. If you want I'll
give you some; It can't be bought with
1. mon-ey. 2. mon-ey. Bless-ed Moth-er
gave it me; Ho-ly, ho-ly love, love.
Pure and good as good can be,_____
Right from heav-en a-bove.

5

Manuscript E
"Peaceful Habitation"

The nearly three hundred songs that make up this manuscript stretch over a time period from 1860 to 1869. It may be the collection of a single scribe, Calvin Miller Fairchild, who had been abandoned when he was two years old near the Church Family dwelling house at Hancock in the early 1840s (fig. 10). In his account of a visit to the Shakers at Hancock, Rev. David MacRae of Scotland wrote of his meeting with the Shaker schoolmaster Calvin Fairchild. MacRae took note of Fairchild's "fair face, his blue eyes that beamed with gentleness, and was not without a pleasant glimmer of half-suppressed merriment (fig. 11).[1]

When Fairchild gave MacRae a history of Ann Lee to read, MacRae found with it a loose paper filled with handwritten verses. These, he learned, were written by Fairchild, who would not let MacRae keep or make copies of them.[2]

According to the last footnote in his account of the Hancock visit, MacRae's book was still in press when he received word that Fairchild had died on December 6, 1869.[3] The date agrees with the death date in the postscript to Manuscript E, which reads, "The foregoing songs were written by Calvin Fairchilds who deceased December 6, 1869, aged 28 years." Did this postscript writer intend "foregoing" to include all the songs or only those immediately preceding? In either case, did the writer mean that Fairchild was the scribe, the composer, or both? What is evident is that at least eleven communities and as many Shaker names are noted as sources of several of the songs. We have identified Hancock (HN) as the provenance of Manuscript E but there is a very real possibility that some or all of the songs in it may have been recorded by another Hancock Shaker or even by a Shaker from another community.

Fig. 10. Portrait believed to be of Calvin Miller Fairchild as a child. PHOTOGRAPH COLLECTION OF HANCOCK SHAKER VILLAGE.

Fig. 11. Replica of the Original Shaker School (c. 1830–1934) at Hancock, Massachusetts. Calvin Miller Fairchild served as schoolmaster in the original structure at the time of Reverend David MaCrae's visit to Hancock in the 1860s. COURTESY JAMES D. OPDAHL.

The manuscript includes many verses with no musical notation, but the majority of the selections are songs scored in small letteral notation. As we have frequently experienced with this notation, there is a dearth of titles and bars, and no staffs.

Six of the thirteen songs we selected from this manuscript are noted songs, in part or throughout. They are rec-ognizable, as described in the preface, by the absence of text in the transcript versions and the insertion of syllables such as "lo, lo, lo" or "lodle, lodle" in the edited versions. Another feature of this manuscript is the inclusion of two hymns, "Whither, O whither on earth can I roam" and "I hear the voice of an angel band," each, as is usual with hymns, having several verses.

Fig. 12. Round Barn at Hancock, Massachusetts, winter 2003. COURTESY JAMES D. OPDAHL.

Shuffling Tune

MS SV–E/HN p. 127

Round in the dance we move, Borne by the gen – tle breez– es,

Cir – cu– la – ting love which Heav – en is be – stow – ing.

Shuffling Tune

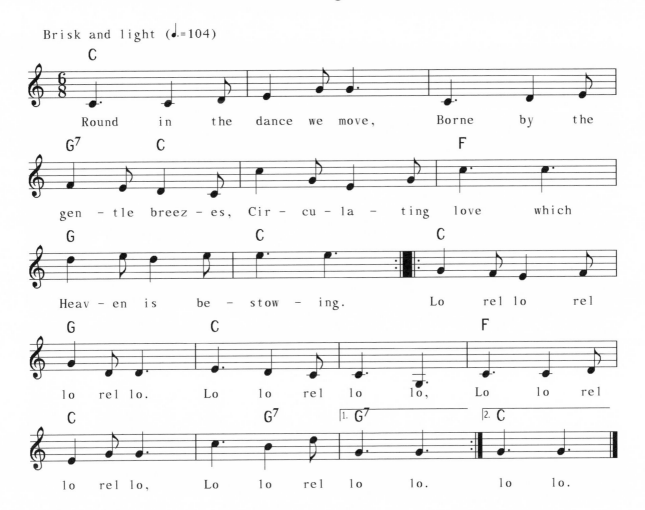

Brisk and light (♩.=104)

Round in the dance we move, Borne by the
gen — tle breez — es, Cir — cu — la — ting love which
Heav — en is be — stow — ing. Lo rel lo rel
lo rel lo. Lo lo rel lo lo, Lo lo rel
lo rel lo, Lo lo rel lo lo. lo lo.

MS SV-E/HN p. 127

Life, life, lib- er- ty, free- dom & sim – plic- i – ty.

Come, come dwell with me in this pres- ent hour.

Life, life, liberty

Joyfully resolute (♩.=120)

Life,   life,   lib - er - ty,   free - dom and   sim -
plic - i - ty!   Come,   come   dwell with me
in   this   pres - ent   hour!_____   Lo   lo
lo - dle lo,   Lo   lo - dle lo   lo,
Lo   lo   lo - lo lo,   Lo   lo - dle lum   lum.

Love

MS SV-E/HN p. 144

It is love that makes the way eas-y O it is

love that makes our path bright Pure love which form-eth our

heav-en Is the es-sence of heav-en-ly light.

It is to the wound-ed a balm which is

sooth-ing The im-press is bless-ed its pow-er di-

vine Like the light of the sun it re-stor-eth the

morn-ing When in dark-ness is shad-owed the mind.

Canterbury.

Love

Brightly (♩.=80)

Canterbury, New Hampshire

It is love that makes the way eas – y;

O it is love that makes our path bright.

Pure_____ love which form – eth our heav – en

Is the es – sence of heav – en – ly light.

It is to the wound – ed_____ a

balm which is sooth – ing. The im – press is

bless – ed; its pow – er di – vine. Like the light of the

sun it re – stor – eth the morn – ing

When, in dark – ness, is shad – owed the mind.

MS SV-E/HN p. 169

(*Sung by Benj. Smith & Co.*)

(Lodle lo lodle lodle lo)

Fast and rhythmical (♩=106)   Sung by Benjamin Smith & Co.

Lo - dle lo lo- dle lo - dle lo lo lo lo, Lo- dle

lo lo lo - dle lo lo lo lo, Lo - dle

lo lo lo lo lo lo lo, Lo - dle

lo lo - dle lo - dle lo - dle lo lo lum.

Lo lo - dle lo lo - dle lo lo - dle lo lo,

Lo lo - dle lo lo - dle lo lo - dle lo lo - dle

Lo lo - dle lo lo - dle lo lo lo lo,

Lo lo - dle lo - dle lo - dle lo lo lum.

MS SV–E/HN p. 183

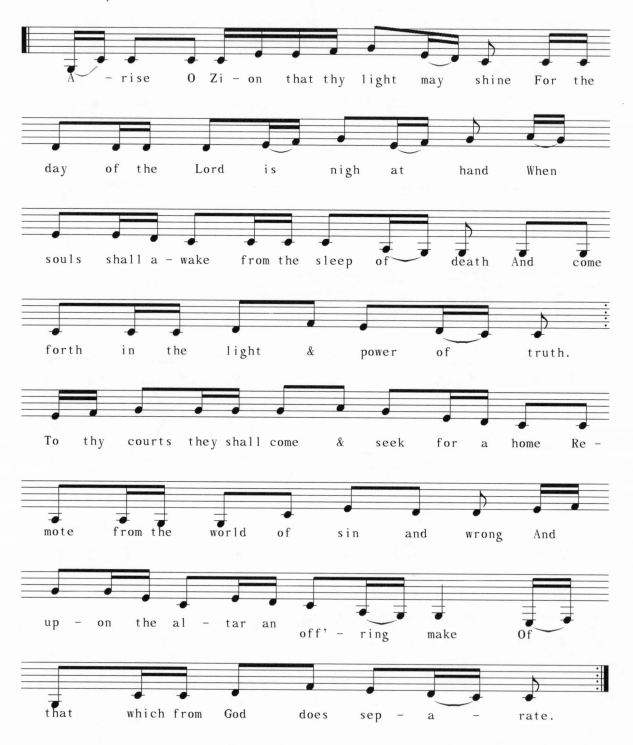

Arise, O Zion

With fervor (♩=72)

A — rise, O Zi - on, that thy light may__ shine; for the
day of the Lord is__ nigh at__ hand, When_
souls shall a - wake from the sleep of__ death, And come
forth in the light and pow'r of__ truth. To thy
courts they shall come and seek for a home Re -
mote from the world of sin and wrong; And up -
on the__ al - tar an off' - ring__ make Of__
that which from God does sep - a - rate.

MS SV-E/HN p. 187

I'll drink at no foun-tain I'll bathe in no stream I'll

wash in no riv - er That will not re - deem

The fur - nace in Zi - on Which cleans - es by fire Is

what my soul cov - ets 'Tis what I de - sire.

Watervliet, Chh.

I'll drink at no fountain

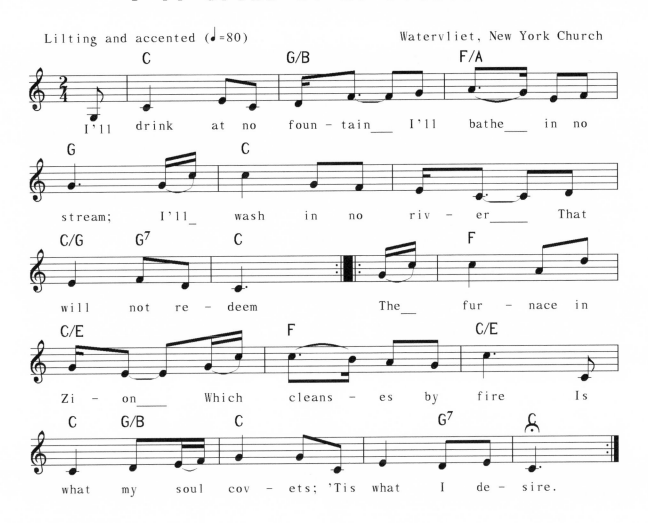

Lilting and accented (♩=80)

Watervliet, New York Church

I'll drink at no foun-tain__ I'll bathe__ in no stream; I'll_ wash in no riv-er____ That will not re-deem The__ fur-nace in Zi-on___ Which cleans-es by fire Is what my soul cov-ets; 'Tis what I de-sire.

MS SV-E/HN p. 188

From the Val – ley to the Mount From the stream – let
to the fount Gos – pel love and friend – ship flow.
'Tis the love of kin – dred souls Will you re – ceive it
here it rolls It is pure and good I know. I know.

(Watervliet)

From the Valley to the Mount

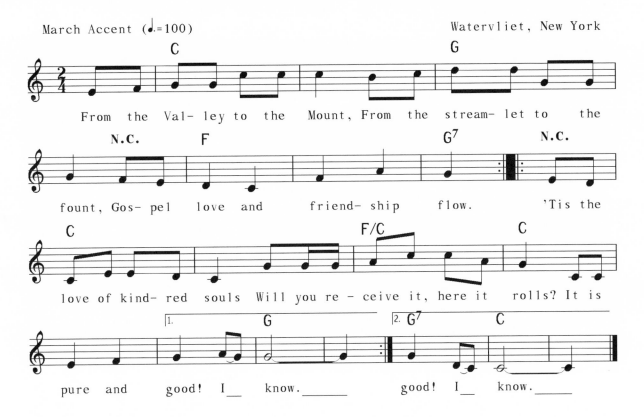

March Accent (♩.=100)   Watervliet, New York

From the Val-ley to the Mount, From the stream-let to the fount, Gos-pel love and friend-ship flow. 'Tis the love of kind-red souls Will you re-ceive it, here it rolls? It is pure and good! I_ know._____ good! I_ know._____

MS SV-E/HN p. 188

Come_ tune up your notes of praise

Sound glo — ry al — le — lu — ia He who called us

can us raise To glo — ry al — le — lu — ia.

(Chh. Watervliet.)

Come, tune up your notes of praise

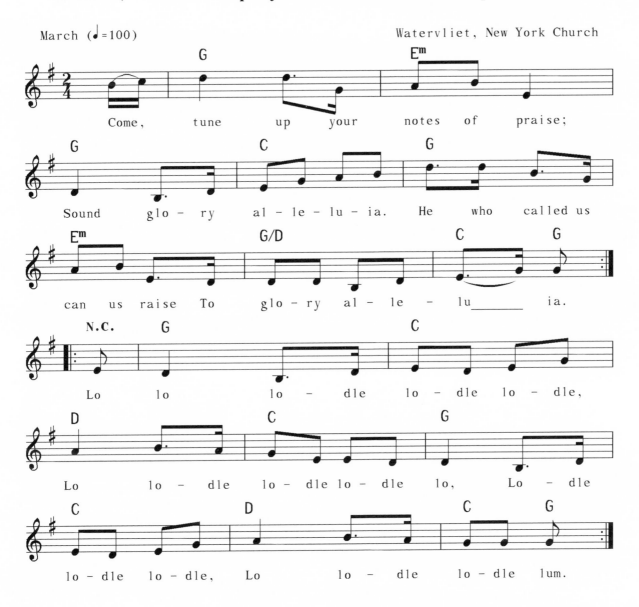

MS SV-E/HN p. 191

We'll We'll raise raise the ban-ner high And

shout a-loud the vic-t'ry's nigh

We'll praise praise our

Lord and King And in tri-umph loud-ly sing.

(I. L. J. Hancock Chh.)

We'll raise, raise the banner high

I. L. J.
Hancock, Massachusetts

Triumphantly (♩=100)

We'll raise, raise the ban - ner high And shout a - loud the vic - t'ry's nigh. Lo - dle lo lo - dle lo - dle lo, Lo - dle lo lo - dle lo lo We'll praise, praise our Lord and King And, in tri - umph, loud - ly sing. Lo lo lo - dle lo - dle lo lo - dle lo - dle lo lo We'll lum.

MS SV–E/HN p. 191

From the scenes of earth I go

To a hap – py hap – py clime Far be – yond this

vale of woe Leav – ing earth – ly joys be – hind.

From the scenes of earth I go

Leisurely (♩.=80)

From the scenes of earth_ I go To a hap - py, hap - py clime, Far be - yond this vale of woe, Leav - ing earth - ly joys be - hind. Lo - dle lo - dle lo - dle lo, Lo - dle lo - dle lo - dle lo, Lo - dle lo - dle lo - dle lo lo, Lo - dle lo - dle lo lum lum.

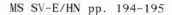

MS SV-E/HN pp. 194-195

Whith − er O whith − er on earth can I roam To

find me an − oth − er such beau − ti − ful home Such

beau − ti − ful home Such beau − ti − ful home To

find me an − oth − er such beau − ti − ful home

Where peace love and un − ion to − geth − er com − bine To

make earth an E − den in this home of mine In

this home of mine In this home of mine To

make Earth an E − den in this home of mine

Worthless are mine of the bright sparkling gem
The riches of Kings or their proud diadems
And worthless is fame with its brilliant array
All worthless compared to our Mother's pure way

All are but wiles of the world to decoy
To dazzle a moment and then to destroy
They're Apples of Sodom all fair to the sight
But inwardly rotten and bitter and blight

Here in the home of the lowly I'll stay
Nor wonder alone in the wide world away
Where waes of temtation incessantly roll
And snares of the wicked are set for the soul

Whither, O whither on earth can I roam

With graceful motion (♩=106)

1. Whith-er, O whith-er on earth can I roam To
2. Worth-less are mine of the bright spark-ling gem, The
3. All are but wiles in the world to de-coy, To
4. Here in the home of the low-ly I'll stay, Nor

find me an-oth-er Such beau-ti-ful home, Such
rich-es of kings or their proud di-a-dems; And
daz-zle a mo-ment and then to de-stroy; They're
wan-der a-lone in the wide world a-way Where

beau-ti-ful home, Such beau-ti-ful home; To
worth-less is fame with its bril-liant ar-ray; All
Ap-ples of Sod-om all fair to the sight, But
waves of temp-ta-tion in ces-sant-ly roll, And

find me an-oth-er such beau-ti-ful home?
worth-less com-pared to our moth-er's pure way.
in-ward-ly rot-ten and bit-ter and blight.
snares of the wick-ed are set for the soul.

home? Where peace, love and un-ion To-geth-er com-
way.
blight.
soul.

bine to make earth an E-den in this home of mine, In

this home of mine, In this home of mine; To

make Earth an E-den in this home of mine? mine?

-81-

MS SV-E/HN pp. 195-196

I hear the voice of an an- gel band Say- ing praise the Lord Your Mak — er While the sun — beams ear — ly light thy land O Youth de – fer not la — ter Com — mence thy jour- ney with a thank- ful lay And praise the Lord thro the well Spent day.

Intense as light of the sun at noon
In thy course like a mighty river
Tho' Storms and Tempests in darkness gloom
So be thy strength and vigor
Renew thy journey with a joyful lay
And praise the Lord thro' the well Spent day

When toils of earth with thee shall cease
And thy sun doth set in splendor
While the evening breeze speaks thy release
Then earth to earth we render
Creation join in a peaceful lay
And praise the Lord thro' eternal day.

Henry Hollister

I hear the voice of an angel band

Stately (♩=80)

Henry Hollister

1. I hear the voice of an an - gel band Say - ing, Praise the Lord, Your__ Mak - er. While the sun - beams ear - ly light thy land, Youth, de - fer__ not la - ter. Com - mence thy jour - ney with a thank - ful lay And praise the Lord thro' the well - spent__ day.

2. In - tense as light of the sun at noon In thy course like a might - y__ riv - er, Tho'__ storms and temp - ests in dark - ness gloom, So be thy strength and vi - gor. Re - new thy jour - ney with a joy - ful lay And praise the Lord thro' the well - spent__ day.

3. When toils of earth with __ thee shall cease And thy sun doth set in__ splen - dor, While the eve - ning breeze__ speaks thy re - lease. Then earth to earth__ we rend - er. Cre - a - tion join____ in a peace - ful lay And praise the Lord thro' e - ter - nal____ day.

MS SV-E/HN p. 204-205

Our love nev – er end – ing no dis – tance can sev – er Un –
bound– ed to you may it flow on for– ev – er This
pure gos – pel un – ion will ev – er re – main; Fare –
well lov – ing friend till we meet you a – gain.

Our love never ending

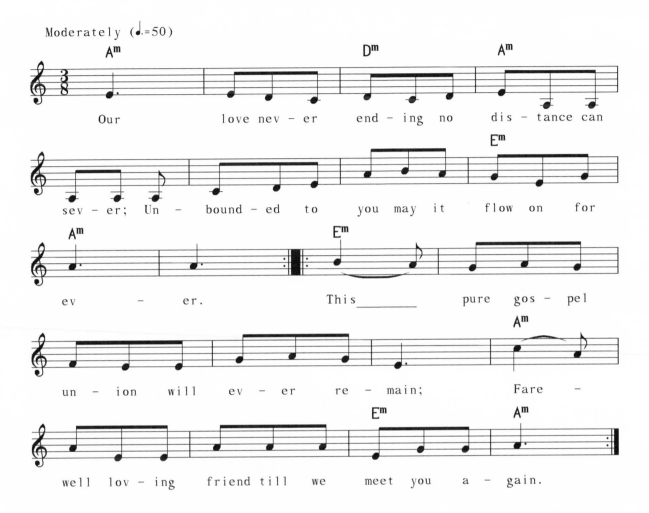

Moderately (♩.=50)

Our love nev – er end – ing no dis – tance can
sev – er; Un – bound – ed to you may it flow on for
ev – – er. This_____ pure gos – pel
un – ion will ev – er re – main; Fare –
well lov – ing friend till we meet you a – gain.

6

Manuscript F

"Tho Life's Morn Rose Bright and Cloudless"

This manuscript evokes memories of leafing through its pages in Brother Ricardo Belden's presence and pausing to jot down his comments whenever we came to a song that had a special context for him. During one of these informal sessions, Brother Ricardo identified "My soul loves to walk in the valley low" as a slow march, "Come to Zion" as a fast march, and "With joy we chant" as a welcome song to be sung with heartfelt warmth in the voice.

Both Brother Ricardo and Russel Haskell, the manuscript's scribe, had resided at the Enfield, Connecticut, community at a time when Haskell (1801–1884) was in the last decade of his life and Brother Ricardo was still a youth. Haskell designed cursive letteral notation and used it to meticulously record every song in this manuscript.

In reviewing the songs with Brother Ricardo, it became apparent that not all of the songs in the manuscript were dated. Those that were had dates that fell in the 1870s. Daniel Patterson noted that although Haskell had devised cursive notation earlier and had used it from time to time, it seems that he employed a revised format in his 1870s manuscript books with much greater frequency than at any time previously (fig. 14). Patterson also drew attention to the fact that "no other scribe used it."[1] What also helps to identify the manuscript as Haskell's is his distinctive handwriting, the use of cursive notation, and Brother Ricardo's affirmation that the songs were, indeed, entered by Haskell.

Haskell entered all 160 songs in this manuscript without staffs, inserted measure bars in only one ("To the land of the blest"), and assigned titles to only eight. In many instances, Haskell's small, precise handwriting allowed as many as two

songs, and parts of another, on a single page. He assigned modal signs to every song and drew very distinct undulating lines to separate songs from each other. Haskell, like a number of other scribes, used variant spellings. For example, he used *moulding,* a variant of molding, in "Ever changing, ever

Fig. 13. Brethren Shop, Hancock, Massachusetts. Brother Ricardo built and repaired clocks here until declining membership and advancing age necessitated relocating many such activities to the dwelling house. COURTESY JAMES D. OPDAHL.

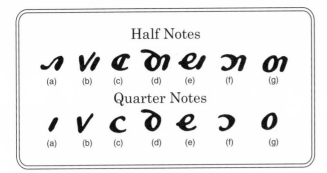

Fig. 14. Russel Haskell's revised cursive letteral notation (1871).
DRAWN BY STEVE SHERMAN FROM SONG NOTES IN MANUSCRIPT F.

aiming," and *wordly,* an obsolete form of worldly, in two songs, "I see a light, and angels bright" and "Tho wordly elements combine."

The songs are mainly *extra*—Brother Ricardo, like Haskell, called such songs "standing." These songs, including the one singled out by Brother Ricardo, "I cannot serve the living God," were sung between dances. This provided the dancers with a much needed respite from the strenuous dance sessions. The manuscript also contains a two-versed hymn," Send, O Lord, thy holy power," in which the composer, like those who wrote A 10, "I will be free, I'll not be bound," and A 21, "Little Big I," in Manuscript A, asks that haughtiness and pride be struck down.

Of the twenty-five songs we chose from this manuscript, several were composed in what came to be called the "Shaker minor." Examples of such songs are "Tho life's morn rose bright and cloudless," "Life, life, living zeal," "The world I've forsaken," "Gird on the heav'nly armor," "O thou my soul, arise and sing," "Come arise, be of good cheer," and "Come to Zion." According to their own writings, Haskell and Youngs had no trouble agreeing that there are two keys, major and minor, both with tonic scales. In almost identical wording, they described the relationship between the tonic and its third for each key and agreed that the major always begins on C. Then, they parted ways. Haskell went on to say that the minor key "always commences on D,"[2] but Youngs wrote that the minor key "commences on A."[3] The latter we know as the aeolian mode. Haskell's definition of the scale, DEFGABCD, is known as the Shaker minor, a unique identification for the commonly known *dorian* mode.

When the Enfield community closed in 1918, the surviving members, including Brother Ricardo, moved to Hancock along with a share of their material possessions. Might this manuscript book have been one of those possessions?

MS SV-F/**EC-13** p. 1

Tho life's morn rose bright and cloudless

Plaintively (♩=112)

Tho life's morn rose bright and cloud - less
And__ the sun did bril - liant ap - pear,
There may be a fear - ful__ temp - est,
Ere the noon__ of life draw- eth near.
Then stand firm__ as the rock of a - ges,
Tho the fierc - est of winds may blow, The
light that il - lum'd thy ear - ly morn - ing A -
gain will ap - pear__ ere the eve - ning__ close.

MS SV–F/**EC–13** p. 2

The stars will not fade

Flowing (♩.=69)

The stars will not fade in their beau - ty____ Nor the
sun will his splen- dor with – hold;_____ Al - tho
some may fail of their du - ty,_____ While
o – thers their birth – right have sold._____
The rem - nant of Is – rael shall pros - per In
strength_____ and in length of their days. The
prom – ise of God will not fal - ter._____ To
those who his true laws o – bey._____

MS SV-F/**EC-13** p. 4

Whence comes the hope that fills my soul? Whence
comes the love I feel? Whence comes the pow'r that
stays my feet In dark temp - ta - tion's hour?
Say not to me, these come by chance, Nor
breathe the pois' nous doubt. My God, he lives;
I know his care; His love is round a - bout.

Whence comes the hope

Strong accent on first beat (♩=120)

Whence__ comes the hope_____ that__

fills my soul?_____ Whence comes the love I__

feel? Whence come the pow'r_____ that

stays my feet_____ In__ dark tem - ta - tion's

hour? Say__ not to me,_____ these

come by chance,____ Nor__ breathe the pois' - nous

doubt. My__ God, he lives I know his

care; His__ love is round a - bout.

MS SV-F/**EC-13** p. 13

Life, life, liv - ing zeal, Free - dom, ho - ly pow - er

Come, come, dwell with me In this pres - ent hour.

Life, life, living zeal

Sung by Brother Ricardo Belden
at Shaker Village, New Lebanon, N. Y.

With a joyous lilt (♩.=108)

Life, life, liv- ing zeal, Free - dom, ho - ly pow - er

Come, come, dwell with me In this pres - ent

hour.___ Lo lo lo -dle lo, Lo lo lo- dle lo,

Lo lo lo - dle lo, Lo lo- dle lo lo.

Detachment is very pronounced; give each word breathing space. No legato!
This song, with some variations and accompanied by instructions for a Shaker
dance, also appears in section 10.

MS SV–F/**EC–13** p. 25

With joy we chant the wel - come strain, Our

lov - ing friends are home a - gain.

What can we say, what can we

do, To make it feel like home to you? to you?

We have no or - gan down this way, And no french

horn on which to play; But we have hearts both

kind and true, That beat the wel - come now for you.

You're wel - come wel - come to our home in the val - ley,

wel - come wel - come wel - come home. wel - come home.

En. Ct. Ch.

With joy we chant

With a joyful lilt (♩.=♩=100)　　　　　　　Enfield, Connecticut Church

MS SV-F/**EC-13** p. 33

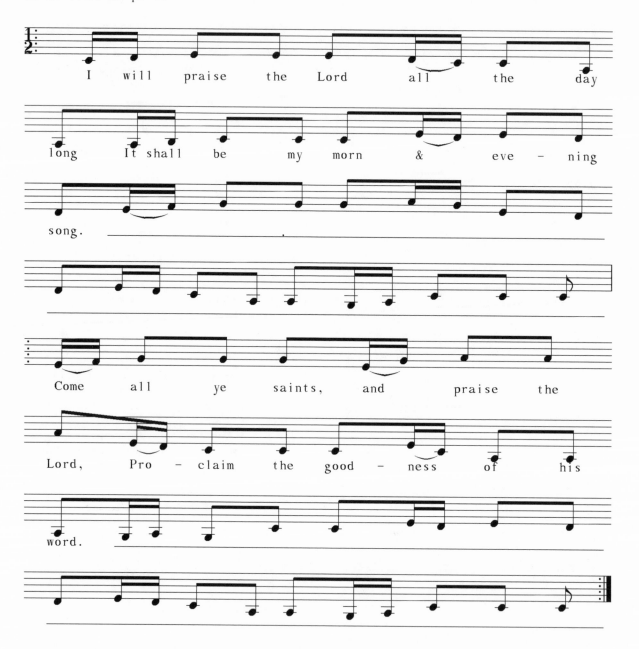

I will praise the Lord

Strong accent on first beat (♩=72)

I will praise the Lord all the day long. It shall be my morn and evening song. Lo-dle lo lo lo lo-dle lo lo lo, Lo-dle lo lo lo lo-dle lo lo lo.

Come all ye saints and praise the Lord, Proclaim the goodness of his word. Lo-dle lo lo lo lo-dle lo lo lo, Lo-dle lo lo lo lo-dle lo lo lo.

MS SV–F/**EC–13** p. 38

1

The world I've for - sak - en with all its vain
pleas - ure: My earth - ly re - la - tion I'm
leav - ing be - hind, To seek in the
gos - pel a dur - a - ble treas - ure, The
great - est of bless - ings that mor - tals can find.
And here in mount Zi - on I've fa - thers &
moth - ers, And of ev' - ry bless - ing an
am - ple sup - ply. Yea here I've found
man - y kind sis - ters & broth - ers, With
whom I am read - y to live or to die. − *En. Ch.*

The world I've forsaken

Swayingly (♪=184)

Enfield Church

The world I've for- sak- en with all its vain pleas- ure; My earth- ly re- la- tion I'm leav- ing be- hind, To_____ seek in the gos- pel a dur- a- ble treas- ure, The great- est of bless- ings that mor- tals can find. And here in Mount Zi- on I've fa- thers and moth- ers, And of ev'- ry bless- ing an am- ple sup- ply. Yea, here I've found man- y kind sis- ters and broth- ers, With whom I am read- y to live or to die.

MS SV-F/**EC-13** p. 39

A - bove the en - chant - ing al - lure - ments of earth, My spir - it is call'd to rise, To seek a bright treas- ure of dur - a - ble worth, That's gain'd by the pure and the wise. wise. I'll ev - er be found with this truth- lov - ing band, Whose mot - to is right o - ver wrong; Who're trav'- ling to heav - en that beau- ti - ful land, Tri - um - phant- ly sing - ing the con - quer- or's song. song.

Above the enchanting allurements

Swayingly (♩.=60)

A - bove the en - chant- ing al - lure- ments of earth, My
spir- it is called to rise,__ To seek a bright treas- ure of
dur- a - ble worth, That's gain'd by the pure and the
wise.____ wise. I'll ev - er be found with this
truth lov - ing band, Whose mot- to is right o - ver wrong; Who're
trav'- ling to heav- en, that beau- ti - ful land, Tri -
um - phant- ly sing- ing the con- quer- or's song.

MS SV–F/**EC–13** p. 42

I see a light, and angels bright

MS SV–F/EC–13 p. 45

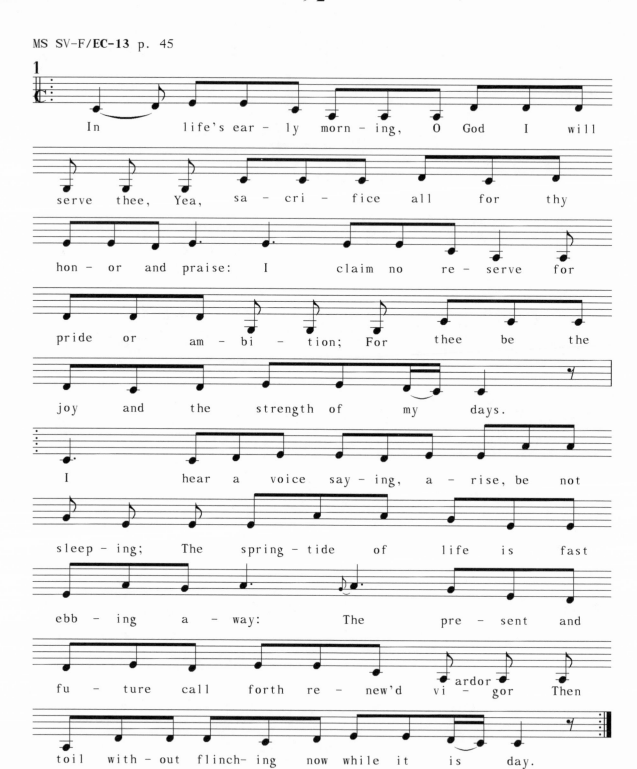

En. Ct. Ch.

–92–

In life's early morning

Enfield, Connecticut Church

Resolutely (♩.=54)

In life's ear-ly morn-ing, God I will serve thee, Yea, sa-cri-fice all for thy hon-or and praise. I claim no re-serve for pride or am-bi-tion, For thee be the joy and the strength of my days. I hear a voice say-ing, a-rise, be not sleep-ing; The spring-tide of life is fast ebb-ing a-way. The pre-sent and fu-ture call forth re-new'd 1.vi-gor; Then toil with-out flinch-ing now while it is day. 2.ar-dor

MS SV-F/**EC-13** p. 45

5

Tho word – ly el – e – ments com– bine, And strive my course to stay, I would not halt in ling' – ring doubt, Nor make the least de – lay. My pre – cious faith in earn – est tones, The pow'r of death de – fies: With cour – age brave, & truth my shield, I'll win the prom – ised prize.

Tho worldly elements combine

MS SV–F/**EC–13** p. 49

Gird on the heav'n- ly ar – mor; Like val – iant sold – iers stand A – gainst the pow'rs of e – vil, Now spread- ing o'er the land. O be not dis- may'd, tho dark may seem the day. The light of truth will shine a – round, And drive the clouds a- way.

Gird on the heav'nly armor

Vigorously (♩.=100)

Gird on the heav'n-ly ar-mor; Like

val – iant sold-iers stand A – gainst the pow'rs of

e – vil, Now spread-ing o'er_ the land. O

be not dis – may'd, tho dark may seem the day. The

light of truth will shine a-round, And drive the clouds a – way.

MS SV-F/**EC-13** p. 50

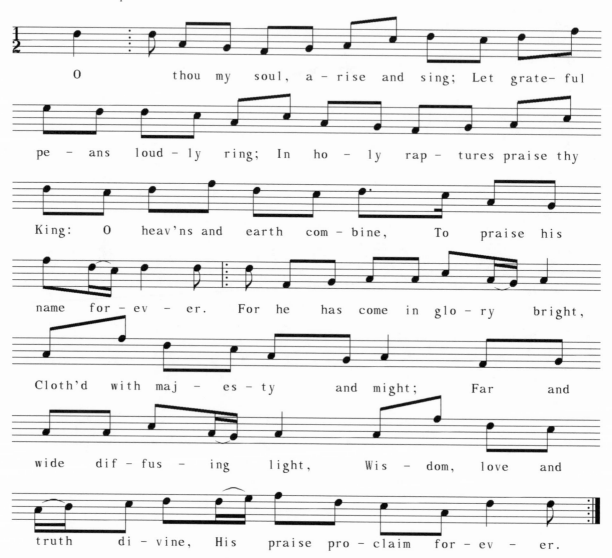

O thou my soul, a-rise and sing; Let grate-ful

pe - ans loud-ly ring; In ho-ly rap-tures praise thy

King: O heav'ns and earth com-bine, To praise his

name for-ev - er. For he has come in glo-ry bright,

Cloth'd with maj - es-ty and might; Far and

wide dif-fus - ing light, Wis - dom, love and

truth di - vine, His praise pro-claim for-ev - er.

C. M. Fairchild.

O thou, my soul, arise and sing

In praise (♩=92)

C. M. Fairchild

O thou, my soul, a – rise and sing; Let

grate– ful pae –ans loud – ly ring; In ho — ly rap – tures

Praise thy King. O heav'ns and earth com– bine To praise his

name for – ev – er. O name for – ev – er. For

he has come in glo – ry___ bright,

Cloth'd with maj – es – ty and might; Far and wide dif –

fus – ing _ light, Wis – dom, love, and

truth di – vine; His_ praise pro– claim for – ev – er.

MS SV–F/**EC-13** p. 60

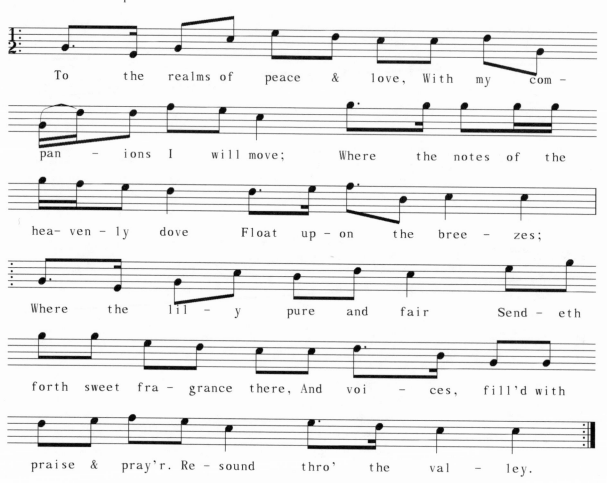

To the realms of peace & love, With my com-

pan - ions I will move; Where the notes of the

hea- ven - ly dove Float up - on the bree - zes;

Where the lil - y pure and fair Send - eth

forth sweet fra - grance there, And voi - ces, fill'd with

praise & pray'r. Re - sound thro' the val - ley.

To the realms of peace and love

Gently moving (♩=72)

To the realms of peace and love, With my com-pan-ions I will move; Where the notes of the heav-en-ly dove Float up-on the bree-zes; Where the lil-y pure and fair, Send-eth forth sweet fra-grance there, And voic-es, filled with praise and pray'r. Re-sound thro' the val-ley.

MS SV-F/**EC-13** p. 63

Come a – rise, be of good cheer; For
lo the an – gels gath – er near, In –
vit – ing us to per – se – vere, And
press in – to the king – dom.

Come arise, be of good cheer

Joyfully (♩.=112)

Come a-rise, be of good cheer; For lo the an-gels gath-er near, In-vit-ing us to per-se-vere, And press in-to the king-dom. Lo lo lo-dle lo-dle, Lo lo lo-dle lo-dle, Lo lo lo-dle lo, Lo lo-dle lum lum.

MS SV–F/**EC–13** p. 67

Not one spar - row is for - got- ten; E'en the
ra - ven God will feed; And the li - ly of the
val- ley, Heav - en grant its ev' - ry need.
Then shall I not trust thee, Fa - ther, In thy
mer - cy have a share? And thru faith & pray'r, my
Moth- er, Mer - it thy pro - tect - ing care?

Not one sparrow is forgotten

MS SV-F/**EC-13** p. 69

I can - not serve the liv - ing God, I can - not serve at all, Un - less with- in my soul there's love For my most ho - ly call. He claims my life, a will - ing heart, A liv - ing sa - cri - fice. I give the whole to gain his love, Which most of all I prize.

I cannot serve the living God

MS SV-F/**EC-13** p. 69

My soul loves to walk in the val – ley low Where the

beau- ti – ful fruits of the gos – pel grow; Where

all dis – cord – ant feel – ings flee; And a

still small voice reigns tri – um – phant – ly.

This is wis – dom's vale where is joy & de – light Her

paths are peace, and her bur – dens light; And

tho heav – y winds and tem – pests as – sail, They

can – not lay waste this beau – ti – ful vale.

My soul loves to walk

MS SV-F/**EC-13** p. 78

When I come to wor – ship thee, O God of lib – er– ty, Give me life and strength to be Not bound not bound. O this liv – ing pow'r be– stow; That each heart may feel & know, Waves of in – spi– ra – tion flow All a– round all a– round.

When I come to worship thee

or

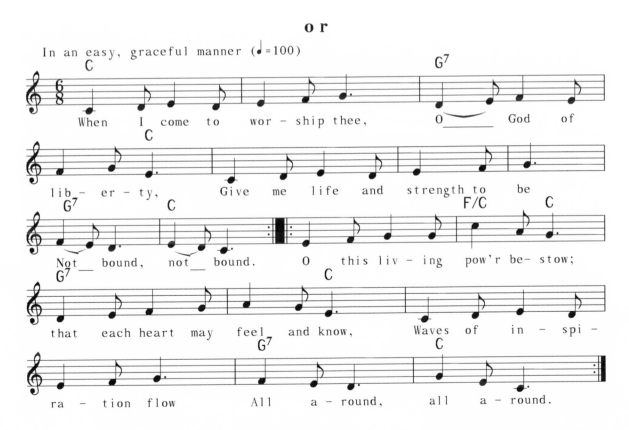

MS SV-F/**EC-13** pp. 84-85

To the land of the blest, to the home of the

free, Where my fa − thers & moth − ers have

gone, I am up − ward bound, and thru faith I can

see The light of an e − ter − nal morn.

Bless− ed home, hap− py home! Tis with

joy that I la − bor for thee. And my heart re − sponds to the

spir − its call; I am liv− ing the life of the free.

Canaan, N. Y.

To the land of the blest

Uplifting (♩=100–112)

Canaan, New York

Bless- ed home,_____ hap- py home,_____ 'tis with joy that I la - bor for thee; And my heart re - sponds to the spir - it's call; I am liv- ing the life__ of the free.

MS SV-F/**EC-13** p. 86

Send, O Lord, thy ho - ly pow - er,

Send, O send it to my soul. Guard & keep me

in each hour, When temp - ta - tions round me roll.

Bow and bend my haugh - ty spir - it;

Bow me down be - fore thy throne: May my soul be

tru - ly hum - ble; Then my off'- rings thou wilt own.

H. Mt.

Send, O Lord, thy holy power

Prayerfully (♩=52)

Holy Mount

Send, O Lord, thy ho - ly pow - er;

Send, O send it to my soul. Guard and keep me

in each hour,___ When temp - ta - tions round me roll.

Bow and bend my haugh - ty spir - it;

Bow me down be - fore thy_ throne; May my soul be

tru - ly hum- ble; Then my off'- rings thou wilt own.

MS SV–F/**EC-13** p. 89

Ever changing, ever aiming

MS SV-F/**EC-13** pp. 90-91

Come to Zi - on, come to Zi - on, Sin - sick souls in

sor - row bound. Lay your cares up - on the al - tar,

Where true heal - ing may be found Shout Al - le -

lu - ia, Al - le - lu - ia; Praise re - sounds o'er

land & sea, All who will, may come and share the

glo - ries of this ju - bi - lee.

Come to Zion

–106–

MS SV–F/**EC–13** p. 93

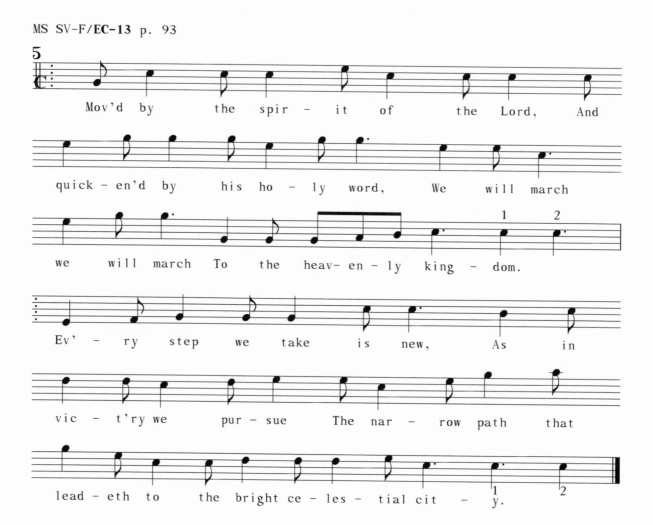

Mov'd by the spirit of the Lord

Brisk march (♩=112)

Mov'd by the spir- it of the Lord, And quick- en'd by his ho- ly word, We will march, we will march To the heav- en- ly king – dom. king – dom. Ev' – ry step we take is new, As in vic – t'ry we pur – sue The nar – row path that lead – eth to the bright ce – les – tial cit – y.

MS SV-F/**EC-13** p. 96

No half-way work, no vain pre-tense Can
sat-is-fy my soul: I want to know I
have full pow'r, Each pas-sion to con-trol.
A lit-tle cross borne part the time, A-
gainst some spe-cial sin, Is not what I'm con-
tent-ed with, But vic-t'ry full I'll win.

No half-way work

7

Manuscript G
"Listen O Listen to Our Humble Prayer"

The scribes used standard (round) notation placed on staffs for songs in this manuscript, but many other features of this notation are lacking. Text does not always match corresponding notes, and words of more than one syllable have no hyphens. In spite of these shortcomings, however, there is no difficulty in determining the scribe's intent on text and note coordination, for all of the songs are very legible. Just two dates, 1887 and 1888, appear on a few songs. New Lebanon and Canaan are the only locations cited and, then, only once each. Over half of the songs in this manuscript are hymns having both clefs and two or more verses.

One of the songs we selected from this manuscript is "I'm glad I am a Shaker" (fig. 16). William Pillow and his family, who had joined the Shakers at New Lebanon for a few months in 1846, kept a journal in which he described a meeting at which the Shakers sang this song.

> December 19—Removed from the North cottage to the Second House and took supper with the family for the first time. May I find oneness with Christ's people and with him. . . . This evening at meeting, Elizbh Bullard expressed her desire to be like God; that is, good. She expressed her thankfulness for having those elder than herself to reprove her and direct her in her way. She then asked Eldress Antoinette if she might be permitted to make a sign expressive of her indignation against all sin and her desire to have it removed from her. She, then, and the whole company shook themselves violently after which was sung "I'm Glad That I Am A Shaker." May I feel a constant abhorrence of all sin and labour continually to be delivered from it.[1]

The diary, in the possession of his great-granddaughter, Marion Pillow Bedell, at the time we had access to it, is a record of the first few weeks the Pillow family resided with the New Lebanon Shakers. Pillow, his wife, and their children began life with the Shakers on 15 November 1846. He enrolled his three sons in the Shaker school and indentured them to Edward Fowler, trustee of the Church family. It took five weeks for William Pillow to move from recording his admiration for Shaker belief to expressing doubts about his religious convictions. The entries ceased on 19 January 1847. It seems that "I'm glad I am a Shaker" no longer held attraction!

Fig. 15. Ministry Shop, Hancock, Massachusetts. Beginning in the 1870s, ministry shops served as dwelling houses and work sites for the ministry, the top governing authority of Shaker society. COURTESY JAMES D. OPDAHL.

Fig. 16. "I'm glad I am a Shaker." Standard notation (Manuscript G).

The boys were still with the Shakers in December 1847, but, in the same month, they left and were taken by their father to New York City. Edward Fowler, to whom the boys had been bound, sued. The court case (1848) pitted the legality of a signed indenture agreement against the sanctity of the family. Ultimately, the judge allowed the three boys to decide their own immediate future. The two youngest chose to be with their father, the oldest to remain with the Shakers. This judicial decision, about which Marian Bedell spoke to us directly in 1955, is also described in Carol Weisbrod's book *The Boundaries of Utopia*.[2]

In a letter written to the oldest son, William Pillow Jr., in 1859, Isaac Youngs of the New Lebanon Shakers tried to dissuade William from pursuing his plans for an upcoming marriage. He wrote, "Thousands of times have I tho't [*sic*] of you since last I saw you and have desired to have some communication, but no time, for more than nine years, has presented itself, so favorable as the present."[3] The date of this letter and the "for more than nine years" reference suggests that William Jr., in spite of his earlier decision to stay with the Shakers, must have left them some time around 1850. It appears that he, like his father, was no longer "glad" to be a Shaker.

MS SV−G/X? p. 7

Oh come ye need – y ones step in! The wa – ters now
are stirred. Ye who would cleanse your souls from
sin. Be not by doubt de – terred. An an – gel of the
Lord is near. To strength – en and to bless, These
wa – ters pure will heal and cheer. All who would
life pos – sess

Jan 1888 M J A

Oh come, ye needy ones

MJA
Jan. 1888

With fervor (♩.=80)

Oh come, ye need-y ones, step in! The
wa - ters now__ are stirred, Ye who would cleanse your
souls from sin Be not by doubt de - terred.__
An an - gel of__ the Lord is near To
strength-en and__ to bless.__ These wa - ters pure will
heal__ and cheer All who would life pos - sess.____

MS SV-G/X? p. 9

Love me, bless me, holy angels

Gently (♩=66)

Love me, bless me, ho- ly an- gels. Let me feel your

quick- 'ning power. Oh, I crave a low- ly spir- it

And your guid- ance ev- ery hour. Give me faith that's

ev- er liv- ing. This will keep me in the way; And bap- tize me,

bless- ed an- gels, Un- to you I humb- ly pray.

−I,m glad I am a Shaker −

MS SV−G/X? p. 21

I,m glad I am a shak - er And num - bered with the flock Who are the true par – tak – ers And found- ed on a rock, My thank- ful- ness I cant ex – press. For this bless- ed day. That I have found such peace & rest, And com – fort in the way

I'm Glad I Am a Shaker

With joy (♩.=92)

I'm glad I am a Shak - er And num - bered with the flock, Who are the true par - tak - ers And found - ed on a rock. My thank - ful - ness I can't ex - press For this bless - ed day That I have found such peace and rest, And com - fort in the way.

MS SV−G/X? p. 141

I love to com − mune with the an − gels

the jus − ti − fied an − gels of God. Their re − cords are

clean from the dark stains of sin And they dwell in a

hap − py a − bode They come to our homes with their

bless − ings To cheer us on the heav − en − ly

road, And fill us with hope that at last we may

dwell With them in their hap − py a − bode

I love to commune with the angels

Joyfully (♩=120)

I love to com - mune__ with the an -
gels, The jus - ti - fied an - gels of
God._____ Their re - cords are clean from the
dark stains of sin; And they dwell in a
hap - py a - bode. They come to our homes with their
bless - ings To cheer us on the heav - en - ly
road; And fill us with hope that at last we may
dwell With__ them in their hap - py a - bode.

8

Manuscript H

"We'll Broaden Our Circle and Let in the Angels"

As in the previous manuscript, songs in this one are written in standard notation. In Jerry Count's 1957 interview with Brother Ricardo, he asked Brother Ricardo about the Shaker system of letteral notation. Brother Ricardo's answer included a reference to the shift to standard notation: "The [letteral] notation was given by inspiration to Elder Giles Avery when he was quite a young man and was used by the societies for many years afterwards. Finally, they turned to [standard or round] notes as you understand them now."[1]

This manuscript is the only one in which some person added one- or two-word notations to identify the nature of most of the songs. For example, of the five songs we selected, this person identified "Songs of victory" as a quick song, "Behold what wonders now we see" and "O earth's fleeting joys" as slow marches, and "Oh come walk with me" as simply a march. He or she left "Oh the river of life" unidentified. The scribe wrote every note with stems up, as we have shown in the transcript copies of the songs. The only dates that appear in this manuscript are 1889 and 1893, and they appear very infrequently. Except for very infrequent references to Canaan (fig. 17) and New Lebanon, the songs lack site identifications.

Fig. 17. Lower Canaan Family Buildings, Mount Lebanon, New York. The Berkshire Industrial Home for Boys has been located on the site since 1884. COURTESY SHAKER MUSEUM AND LIBRARY, OLD CHATHAM, NEW YORK.

MS SV–H/X? p. 13

Slow March

A. W.

Be - hold what won - ders now we see The

li - on and the lamb a - gree The leo - pard with the

kid is fed And by a lit - tle child is led

On moun - tain high or in the vale No

one may hurt, no harm as - sail, For all a - round is

ho - li - ness Un - to the Lord our right - eous - ness.

Behold what wonders now we see

Slow march (♩=80)

A. W.

MS SV−H/X? p. 28

March

M.R.

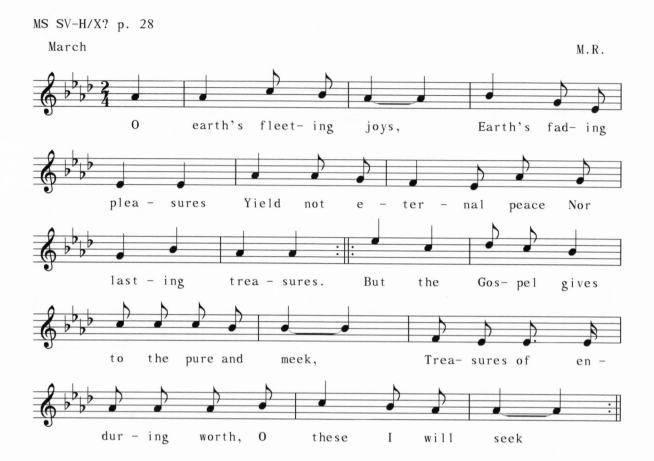

O earth's fleeting joys

March (♩=112)   M. R.

O earth's fleet- ing joys, Earth's fad- ing plea - sures Yield not e - ter - nal peace Nor last- ing trea - sures. trea - sures. But the Gos- pel gives to the pure and meek, Trea- sures of en - dur - ing worth, O these I will seek!

MS SV-H/X? p. 30

March

Eldress Anna

Oh come walk with me of the cup that I

give Drink free - ly each thirst - y soul.

Ye may know of a truth that to die is to

live And if wound - ed to be made whole.

Oh, come walk with me

March (♩=104)

Eldress Anna

Oh,___ come walk with me; of the cup that I give Drink free - ly,_ each thirst - y soul.

Ye may know of a truth that to die is to live And, if wound - ed, to be made whole.

MS SV–H/X? p.40

Quick Song   Second Family

Songs of vic- to – ry the an – gels are sing – ing

Life and lib-er – ty un – to us bring- ing.   Come

let us step   to the mu – sic & song,   With a

tes – ti – mo – ny a – gainst all   wrong.

–115–

Songs of victory

Quick song (♩=76)

Second Family

Songs of vic-to-ry the an – gels are sing – ing;

Life and lib-er-ty un – to us bring – ing.

Come let us step to the mu – sic and song, With a

tes – ti – mo – ny a – gainst all wrong.

-116-

MS SV–H/X? p. 60

Eldress Anna

Oh the riv- er of life that mak - eth glad The

heart of the wear - y the lone and sad, That

wak - ens the soul to a re - so - lute will The

du - ties and cares of each day to ful - fill.

It gushes from moun - tains and flows in the vale It

springs from a foun - tain whose wa - ters ne'er fail, And

who' - ev - er drinks shall thirst nev - er more And

who - ev - er bathes from death t'will re - store.

Oh the river of life

Gently assuring (♩.=72–80)

Eldress Anna

Oh the riv-er of life__ that mak—eth glad The heart of the wear—y, the lone and sad, That__ wak-ens the soul to a re-so-lute will, The du—ties and cares of each day to ful—fill! It__ gush—es from moun—tains and flows in the vale.___ It springs from a foun—tain whose wa—ters ne'er fail; And_ who—ev—er drinks___ shall thirst nev—er more. And who—ev—er bathes, from death t'will re—store.

9

Manuscript I

"The Homeland"

This twentieth-century manuscript is the most recent of the nine manuscripts and the only one in which notes and text are written on commercially preprinted staffs. Brother William H. Perkins of the New Lebanon community entered all of the selections (seven hymns and one song) between November 10, 1914, and January 21, 1915 (fig. 18). Even the time of the day when the hymns and one song were entered is written above some of them. Selections with format akin to that of responsive readings and featuring biblical sayings of Jesus and St. John complement two of the hymns.

We know that the Shakers, particularly in their early history, wrote text to tunes borrowed from outside the Shaker communities. Less usual is a reversal of the pattern; that is, the Shakers borrowing text from an outsider and then setting the borrowed text to music. Such an example in this manuscript is the song "The Death of Lincoln." The title and text of this hymn are that of the poem written by William Cullen Bryant in 1865 following Lincoln's assassination.[1] Biblical writings also serve as texts for hymns in this very sparse document.

We found, in this manuscript, two sets of loose pages that appear to have been torn out of much earlier manuscripts. Only one set has music accompanying the verses. Although out of time sequence, we felt that these two sets of loose pages should stay with the 1914 manuscript where we found them. We chose five songs from the set that includes both text and tune. On the second page of this same set, an unknown scribe wrote "Recorded in this book Oct 25th 1852." The other seven pages of this set have the identical aged appearance, ragged torn edge, notation, handwriting, and layout of the page with the 1852 date.

When someone, Shaker or otherwise, cut the lay-in pages out of their original manuscript, he or she cut them very close to the song content. This caused a loss of a syllable or word in two or three instances, but fortunately the music notes remain intact. The aging of the lay-in pulp-type paper and foxing sometimes necessitated the use of a magnifying glass to read segments of the songs.

Fig. 18. Elder William H. Perkins, Second Family, Mount Lebanon, New York. Perkins, a woodcarver from England, was among the last converts to join the Shakers. COURTESY SHAKER MUSEUM AND LIBRARY, OLD CHATHAM, NEW YORK.

The Death of Lincoln

MS SV-I/NL p. 9
William Cullen Bryant

W. H. P.

Oh,   slow   to   smite and   swift to   spare,   Gen –
In   sor – row   by   thy   bier we   stand,   A –
Thy   task   is   done; the   bond   are   free;   We
Pure   was   thy   life; Its   blood– y   close   Hath

tle   and   mer – ci – ful   and   just!   Who,
mid   the   awe   that   hush– es   all,   And
bear   thee to   an   hon – ored   grave,   Whose
placed   thee with   the   sons   of   light,   A –

in   the   fear   of   God,   didst   bear   The_____
speak   the   an – guish of   a   land   That_____
proud– est   mon – u – ment   shall   be   The_____
mong   the   no – ble   host   of   those   Who_____

ad. iib.

sword.   the   sword of   pow – er,   a   na – tion's trust.
shook,   that   shook with   hor – ror   at   thy   fall.
broken   the   bro – ken   fet – ters of   the   slave.
perished, who   per – ished   in_____   the   cause of   right.

The Death of Lincoln

William Cullen Bryant
Sorrowfully (♩=66)

William H. Perkins

Oh, slow to smite and swift to spare, Gen -
In sor - row by thy bier we stand, A -
Thy task is done; the bond are free; We
Pure was thy life; Its blood- y close Hath

tle and mer - ci - ful and just! Who,
mid the awe that hush- es all, And
bear thee to an hon - ored grave, Whose
placed thee with the sons of light, A -

in the fear of God, didst bear The_____
speak the an - guish of a land That_____
proud- est mon - u - ment shall be The_____
mong the no - ble host of those Who_____

sword. the sword of pow - er, a na - tion's trust.
shook, that shook with hor - ror at thy fall.
broken the bro - ken fet - ters of the slave.
perished, who per - ished in_____ the cause of right.

Harp Song

MS SV–I/NL (Lay–in) pp. 3–4

A - wake wake a - wake my harp and

tune your lays for Moth – er A - wake wake a -

wake my harp and sound her praise for -

ev – er Moth – er's gos – pel will in – crease for

it is pure and ho – ly And her bless – ings

of sweet peace Rest on the meek and low – ly

Harp Song

Farewel Song

MS SV-I/NL (Lay-in) p. 5

May the bless – ings of heav – en like

dews be de – scend – ing On you Moth – er's

child – ren, both now and ev – er – more. And

may you fare – wel in this peace, love and

bless– ing, Un – til we meet on Ca – naan's hap– py

shore. Hap – py shore hap – py shore On the

banks of sweet free– dom, where part– ing is no more.

From N L.

Farewell Song

Sweetly (♩=96)

New Lebanon, New York

May the bless - ings of heav - en like____ dew be de - scend - ing On____ you, Moth - er's child- ren, both now and ev - er - more And____ may you fare - well in this peace, love and bless- ing Un - til we meet on Ca - naan's hap - py shore. Hap - py shore, hap - py shore On the banks of sweet free- dom, where part- ing is no more.

Love from Heaven

MS SV-I/NL (Lay-in) pp. 6-7

from New Lb.

Love from Heaven

Smoothly flowing (♩.=58)

New Lebanon, New York

Here's love sweet – ly flow – ing from Heav- en, from Heav- en; Here's love sweet- ly flow – ing for all who be – lieve. Come gath – er, come gath – er of this bless – ed trea – sure; Come gath – er, come gath – er for all may re – ceive.

Bright Little Gem

MS SV-I/NL (Lay-in) p. 8

Re - ceive my sweet- est love with this

bright lit- tle gem of pure in - no - cence love

joy and peace with an end - less in - crease

I have a pret- ty gem of gold you see I've

brought in my lit - tle bill for thee Twas

gath - ered up from the heav - en - ly mine To

give un - to thee while here in time

Bright Little Gem

Sweet Rest

MS SV-I/NL (Lay-in) p. 8

To those who weep and those who mourn

A prom - ise has been given That

when their work on earth is done They'll

find sweet rest in heaven.

Sweet Rest

10

Beyond the Manuscripts

As already detailed in the foreword and preface, Brother Ricardo Belden not only gave Shaker song manuscripts to Jerry Count, he also taught some Shaker songs and dances to the staff and campers during the early years of Shaker Village. In singing these songs, he used the embellishments and tempos that he remembered from his own past; for some songs, he added dance (or "laboring," as the Shakers called dancing) instruction and gestures. We are very much indebted to Stu Jamieson for reviewing with us detailed descriptions of these particular dance formations, motions, and vocal embellishments. A case in point is the impressive detail found in his instructions for the round dance accompanying "Who Will Bow and Bend."

After leaving Shaker Village, Stu kept Brother Ricardo Belden's teachings alive over the next several decades when

Fig. 19. Chair Factory, South Family, Mount Lebanon, New York. The Shaker Village teenagers and staff built a theater in this building for their public presentations of Shaker songs and dances. AUTHORS' COLLECTION.

presenting Shaker song and dance programs for concert performances. He shared the benefit of these experiences with us by way of more than two dozen visits, letters, phone calls, and e-mail communications between June 1994 and May 2002.

Although Brother Ricardo's variations in song text, his music style, and his particular song and dance combinations may not always follow formats found in other sources, we do feel it is important that we remain true to Brother Ricardo's intent. According to Sybil Count, Brother Ricardo taught the songs and dances, and passed along the manuscripts, with the expressed hope that all would be used in an empathetic way to help enlighten the world's people about the Shakers.[1]

Performing a Shaker dance helps one realize the importance of the "quick" songs—or "standing" songs, as Brother Ricardo, following Russel Haskell's example, called them. These songs were sung between dances by standing singers to provide rest for the Shakers participating in the dances. As a side note, the Shakers were not inflexible in the use of these short songs—they also sang them in worship services, while working, and on special occasions.

The early Shakers engaged in "promiscuous" dancing, meaning that the dances were spontaneous and unstructured in movement and often inspired by a "religious high." At some point during the mid-1780s, a divine revelation inspired Father Joseph Meacham to introduce the idea of using prescribed dance forms rather than the existing promiscuous manner of dancing. The Shakers, believing these structured dances to be spiritual expressions of work honoring God, called them "laboring." There was considerable fluctuation in the degree of interest in laboring in the years between 1787 and 1850. When religious ecstacy ran high,

I'm on my way to Zion

Sung by Brother Ricardo Belden
at Shaker Village, New Lebanon, N. Y.

Joyfully (♩=100)

I'm on my way to Zi - (i)-on, that peace-ful hap-py man - sion, Where life is ev - er flow - ing and death is nev - er known. Come on, my well- be - lov - ed, Ye whom the lord hath sav - ed, Let not your hearts be trou - bled. You'll soon ar- rive at home.

such as during the 1837–1847 decade of spiritual manifestations, a spontaneous reversion during a structured dance to promiscuous dancing was not unusual. Nevertheless, the collection of structured dances and marches that emerged between 1820 and 1850 includes the largest number of significant and impressive examples of Shaker laboring. Throughout the late nineteenth century and into the twentieth, the decline in membership and the aging of the remaining Shakers increasingly led to limiting laboring to the slow marches and to forgoing the demanding and intricate fast dances and marches.

During the short time that William Pillow Sr. lived with the Shakers, he included his observations of laboring meetings in a 20 December 1846 diary entry (see the introduction to section 7). Pillow's description of the scene suggests that he was observing promiscuous dancing. Or had he already become disillusioned enough to interpret even "choreographed" dancing as being promiscuous?

At 2 we had a labour meeting for young believers to practice the manner in which elder Frederick gave an interesting accounting of its being revealed to Father Joseph in a vision. . . . In the evening at 6 had a regular meeting for worship during which Elder Richard expressed his desire for more love, suiting the action to the word he embraced Elder Frederick; then all the brethren embraced one another. Soon after which in marching John Robe was operated on so as to jump about in all directions; then the whole company commenced jumping about in all directions; and irregularly with all their might. This was an extraordinary meeting; and much loving prevailed.[2]

The first song in this section, "I'm on my way to Zion," is a dynamic march. During the late 1940s, elderly townfolk in New Lebanon told Gloria Wagner Jamieson that they remembered hearing this song sung by Shakers who were marching to work in the fields.[3]

Staff and teenagers at Shaker Village found childlike delight in the 1830s song "Ine Vine Violet" and were eager to discover the meaning of the non-English syllables. When questioned by Jerry Count in a recorded interview in 1952, Brother Ricardo explained: "Any song in a seeming foreign language is generally Indian language but some of them are not, but I do not know what language. I do not know that anybody did know what the language was that they were given in at the time. . . . They simply wrote them down as they received them in the religious ceremonies or at other times. . . . They wrote them as they were given without knowing the message in a great many cases. Sometimes the meaning was given a long time afterwards to somebody else in some cases."[4] Andrews identified "Ine Vine Violet" as a

Fig. 20. Workshop, South Family, Mount Lebanon, New York. An overhead walkway connected this building to the chair factory building. The Shaker Village Work Camp used this building as a residence for teenaged boys. AUTHORS' COLLECTION.

nonsense-syllable song.[5] Whether the syllables are nonsense or dialect, young children enjoy this song especially when they can repeat the verse several times and, on each repeat, sing faster and faster. Barbara Pickardt of Woodstock, New York, arranged and choreographed the song with this in mind for a youth chorale concert in 2000.[6]

The third song, "Love, O Love," is a march during which singers motioned "gathering in blessings." Patterson noted that John Robe, later an apostate, received this gift song in 1846.[7] Apostates, persons who joined the Shakers and then later left, were seldom permitted to return, and Robe was among those rebuffed.

Brother Ricardo's version of the last line of the song "Precept on Precept"—"We'll shake and we'll shake in the pure light of God"—differed from the last line used in the same song in Andrew's and Patterson's collections. Andrews' and Patterson's copies read "Yea straight and clear straightness the pure way of God."[8]

The discerning reader will note that three of the seven songs in this section appear in other sections of this book: "Who will bow and bend like a willow" from Manuscript C, "Simple Gifts" ("'Tis a gift to be simple") from Manuscript D, and "Life, life, living zeal" from Manuscript F. The reader may also notice some differences between the manuscript versions of these three songs and the versions sung by Brother Ricardo. We have included dance instructions for these three songs and for "Precept on Precept."

The dances in this section are examples of the structured dances that began making appearances as early as the late eighteenth century. During the first half of the nineteenth century, Shakers modified old ones, if an occasion so de-

Ine Vine Violet

Sung by Brother Ricardo Belden
at Shaker Village, New Lebanon, N. Y.

Fast and lively (♩=120)

I - ne vĪ - nē vi - o - let ē - nē sē - nē vīn - go pret,

Y - fen wa - fen wa - ne voo, O - le mō - lē min - zy two.

A - cren wa - cren wa - ny vō, Moth- er's love is e - ven so,

U - ne e - ne I - ne vā, Now in love we'll dance and play.

Love, O Love

Sung by Brother Ricardo Belden
at Shaker Village, New Lebanon, N. Y.

Fig. 21. View of the South Family Buildings, Mount Lebanon, New York. AUTHORS' COLLECTION.

manded, and created new ones. At the same time, prescribed hand gestures were miming the wording of those songs that accompanied the dances and marches. Even during the years of declining memberships some Shakers, circumstances permitting, continued to use selected gestures as they stepped along in their slow marches.

Brother Ricardo demonstrated two hand gestures, "casting off sins" and "gathering in blessings," for "Life, life, living zeal," "Precept on Precept," and "Who will bow and bend like a willow." If the dance calls for a "casting off sins" gesture, then that gesture is used throughout the dance; the same goes for the "gathering in blessings" gesture. If other miming gestures are called for, such gestures merely interrupt the background pattern of casting or blessing. In either gesture the hands are tightly cupped, the fingers are touching, and the thumbs are touching the sides of the index fingers. The wrists do not flex; all motion takes place at the elbow joint.

When "casting off sins," the palms face down and the hands start about sixty degrees above the horizontal and sweep downward to about thirty degrees below the horizontal. After the downstroke, the upstroke returns the hands to the starting position; the emphasis is on the downward casting motion. Arms remain parallel throughout. When "gathering in blessings," the same sweeping motion occurs, except that the palms face upward and the emphasis is on the upstroke. The motion starts about sixty degrees below the horizontal and ends about thirty degrees above the horizontal, with the arms always remaining parallel to each other.

Shaker Hollow Square Dance Instructions

When starting to perform this dance, the Shaker Brothers and Sisters took positions in the same square or rectangle and maintained open corners in either formation (fig. 22). At the start, the Shaker Brothers lined up, facing to their right, on two adjacent sides of the square or rectangle, and the Sisters lined up, also facing to their right, on the other two ad-

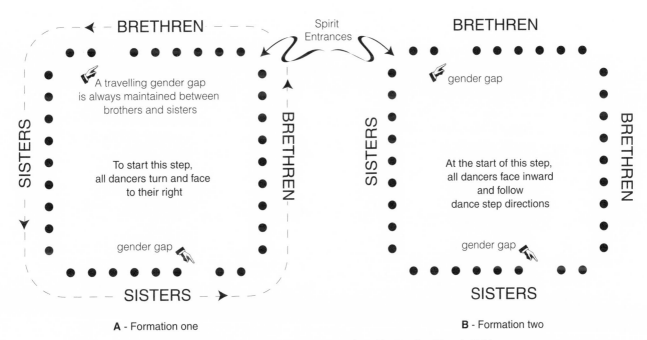

A - Formation one

B - Formation two

Fig. 22. The Hollow Square Dance as remembered by Brother Ricardo Belden.
GRAPHIC BY STEVE SHERMAN.

Life, life, living zeal

Sung by Brother Ricardo Belden
at Shaker Village, New Lebanon, N. Y.

With a joyous lilt (♩.=108)

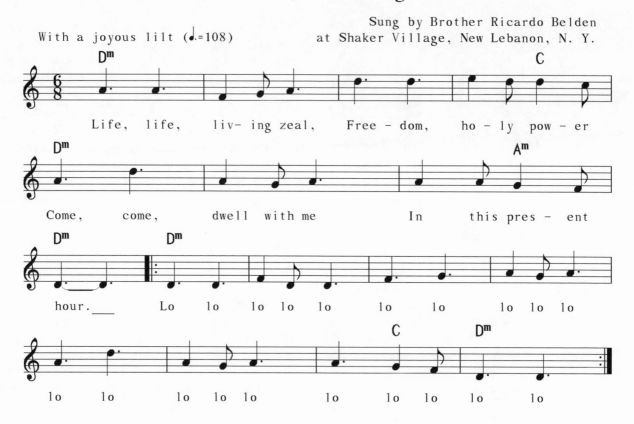

jacent sides. If the room space did not accommodate a square layout, the Shakers resorted to a rectangular formation.

Why did the Shakers maintain open corners in these square or rectangular dance formations? Dan Patterson, responding to a recent inquiry, offered an explanation that prompted a memory in us of a childhood experience. As probably generations of children have done, we used to devise square formations in jest for circle or single-line singing games. It did not take long to discover that classmates adjacent to the corners collided with each other when stepping forward into the square unless the corners were left open. Patterson's explanation for the open corners enlarged on the same phenomenon.[9]

According to Brother Ricardo, breaks at the corners served as invitations to spirits to enter the dance formation and participate if they so wished. To date, we have failed to find any other source that assigns a spiritual use to the corner breaks. Was Brother Ricardo remembering the 1837–1847 decade of "Mother's Work," when spiritual manifestations were prolific? Was he reflecting some very personal inner experience? Were there other Shakers among his acquaintances who supported the same belief? We now regret that we never realized that the concept of "spirit entrances" may have been unique to Brother Ricardo in some way. Our naiveness ran interference with the need for further enlightenment.

To dance to "Life, life," form a square or rectangle as the Shakers did and proceed as instructed through Formation 1 and Formation 2.

Formation 1. During the verse, the dancers move, counter-clockwise, along the perimeter of the square or a rectangle. A "traveling" gender gap is conscientiously preserved throughout the dance. The gender gaps and the corner breaks may coincide in the opening formation but, as the participants dance, the gender gaps "travel" with them and may appear anywhere along the perimeter. While moving forward, the dancers mime the "casting off sin" motion. According to Brother Ricardo's directions, dancers march faster with longer steps past spirit entrances so as not to impede the spirits or get caught at the corners before the verse ends. There is no lingering at the four entrances. At the end of the verse, the dancers stop and face inward.

Formation 2. (a) At the onset of the "lo-lo" section, dancers remain standing on the perimeter of the square or rectangle and face inward. The corners, as in Formation 1, are left open; hands are extended with palms down in the "casting off sin" attitude. On the first "lo," the dancers, in place, jump upward with both feet and, while in mid-jump, move the right foot forward and the left foot back. At the same time, they lower their forearms to the horizontal position of the

"casting off sins" motion. (b) On the next "lo," the dancers, while in place, jump upward and reverse the foot action, moving the right foot back and the left foot forward, and they complete the "casting off sins" motion.

Alternate between (a) and (b) at every "lo." The feet swap positions as the hands sweep downward in unison from the elbows. Note that the motions do not follow the beat; that is, these motions follow the melodic rhythm pattern (i.e., the timing of the "lo") rather than a regular beat pattern. When Stu Jamieson pointed out the relationship between the motions and the melodic rhythm, he added the comment, "A very different thing indeed—and tough!"[10]

Brother Ricardo stressed that the singers should stand in Shaker style to one side during the dance and make a very distinct separation between each word. No legato! In addition, he taught the same vocable, "lo," for all of the wordless notes, indicating the values of the notes by the length of time he lingered on them.

Hollow C March Instructions

Derobigne M. Bennett and Isaac N. Youngs described in their 1 November 1840 journal entry the occasion when the spirits of the founding parents, including Mother Ann Lee, demonstrated walking the heel-to-toe. "The elders spake, that Fr Wm had made known the mind of the heavenly parents, concern-

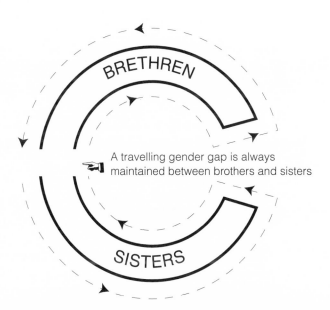

Fig. 23. The Hollow C March as remembered by Brother Ricardo Belden. GRAPHIC BY STEVE SHERMAN.

Precept on Precept

Sung by Brother Ricardo Belden
at Shaker Village, New Lebanon, N. Y.

With confidence (♩.=58)

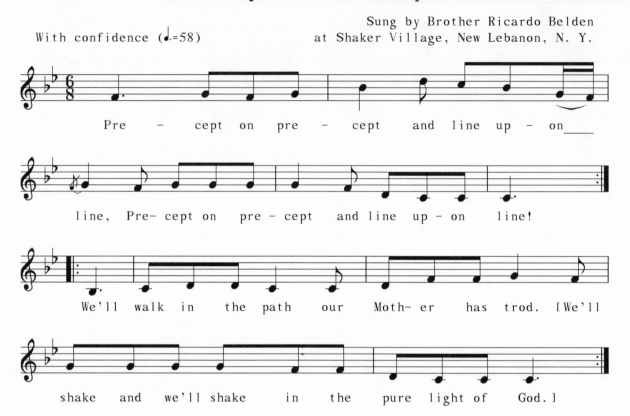

Pre — cept on pre — cept and line up — on___
line, Pre- cept on pre — cept and line up — on line!
We'll walk in the path our Moth- er has trod. [We'll
shake and we'll shake in the pure light of God.]

Fig. 24. South Family Dwelling House, Mount Lebanon, New York. The Shaker Village Camp/Group used it as a residence for teenaged girls. COURTESY SHAKER MUSEUM AND LIBRARY, OLD CHATHAM, NEW YORK.

ing those of us now called together—Fr Wm had brot for each of us a strait and narrow path to walk, it was strait as straitness, no turning to the right nor left. . . . We walked for some time, on the joints of the floor,—& the rest stood by."[11]

Three days later, the spirit of Father James Whitaker introduced words and music for a song to be sung during the narrow path heel-to-toe walk. Over a century later at the Shaker Village Work Camp, Brother Ricardo Belden taught the song as "Precept on Precept." At the same time, he used the Hollow C March as the vehicle for teaching the heel-to-toe manner of walking (fig. 23). He described how the Shakers arranged themselves in the form of a large letter "C" with the outer edge moving in one direction and the inner edge moving in the opposite direction. According to Brother Ricardo, the Brothers lined up, one behind the other, in the curved formation. The Sisters did likewise in the same curved formation. The Brothers and the Sisters observed a discreet "traveling gender gap" between them. (See the explanation of "traveling gap" in the preceding directions for the Hollow Square Dance.) Brother Ricardo added that the Shakers placed their feet heel-to-toe throughout the song. Bennett and Youngs described simple hand-positioning in their journal, but Brother Ricardo remembered the Shakers using the "gathering of blessings" gestures while walking heel-to-toe.[12]

"Simple Gifts": Anecdotes

When Stu Jamieson learned that "Simple Gifts" was one of the songs we were transcribing and editing, he sent an e-mail

to us in which he described how he heard it sung at house concerts almost forty years ago in the Los Angeles area:

During the 1960s when folk music was very popular, Gloria and I attended a house concert in Tarzana, California. The performers were two English folk singers named Jacqui and Bridie, who ran folk clubs including Liverpool Anglican Cathedral. Their concert sticks in my memory for two of the songs they performed that evening, "All God's Critters Have a Place in the Choir," the first time I heard that modern song, and "Simple Gifts." The latter was performed slowly, almost languidly, as was the style common to folk singing then. It was the custom at house concerts to have a "jam session" after the concert itself, wherein the audience could interact musically with the performers. I took advantage of that to speak to both Jacqui and Bridie about the much faster speed with which the Shakers sang "Simple Gifts." I told them about the Shaker dance worship service, and the rationale for religious dancing I had learned from Brother Ricardo Belden. They were fascinated by the subject, so I showed them the Shaker hand gestures for casting off sins and gathering in blessings and demonstrated the steps of the "Square Order Shuffle" dance associated with "Simple Gifts."

Jacqui and Bridie returned to Tarzana for another house concert a year later. During the concert they asked if I was in the audience. I stood, and they then sang "Simple Gifts" at high speed, following that by telling the audience about my instructing them on Shaker dance. They said that they had passed that information on to audiences in the U. K. who were favorably impressed and intrigued by their demonstrations of the hand gestures. They also sang that evening "The Lord of the Dance," which Sydney Carter, the British composer and singer, had written to his adaptation of the tune "Simple Gifts."[13]

After a long search online, Jacqui (Jacqueline McDonald) surfaced in Chester, England, but not Bridie (Bridget Mary O'Donnell), who had passed away. It did not take many conversations with Jacqui to discover that she has long been familiar with the history of Ann Lee's early experiences in nearby Manchester.

Both Jacqui McDonald and Sydney Carter played and sang at the Anglican Cathedral in Liverpool—also nearby—during the early 1960s. Jacqui McDonald told us that when Carter sang "Lord of the Dance" at these concerts, he invited the audience to join him in singing the chorus.[14]

Sydney Carter, in adapting the "Simple Gifts" tune, was connecting with the age-old practice of using dance as an expression of religious feelings. "Simple Gifts" is, after all, a song to which the Shakers danced. In addition, "Lord of the

Simple Gifts

Sung by Brother Ricardo Belden
at Shaker Village, New Lebanon, N. Y.

Quick dance (♩=120-130)

'Tis the gift to be sim-ple; 'Tis the gift to be free. 'Tis the

gift to come down where we ought to be. And_

when we find our-selves in the place just right, 'Twill

be in the val – ley of love and de – light.

When true sim – plic-i – ty is gained, To

bow and to bend we shan't be a – shamed. To

turn, turn will be our de – light; Till by

turn – ing, turn – ing we come around right.

Dance" echoes the medieval practice of overlaying traditional secular dance songs with Christian religious themes. This medieval practice grew out of a need to use the familiar as a base for the new in order to more easily gain converts. Evelyn Kendrick Wells, commenting on this need in her book *The Ballad Tree,* wrote "The transference of this strongly entrenched song-dance from the secular to the sacred is one more instance of the use by religious reformers of a folk custom on which to build a better life for the people."[15] An example is the medieval song "My Dancing Day," in which aspects of the secular dance were combined with a Christian theme centering on the life of Jesus.[16] The Shakers were not the first to combine song and dance with religious worship!

"Simple Gifts": The Embellishments of Brother Ricardo

Youngs used the terms "diminutive note" and "long note" rather than "grace note" and "main note" and defined the appoggiatura as a "transition showing a short graceful slide from one note to another."[17] Some Shaker scribes actually inserted miniature notes to indicate the slide when they recorded songs in manuscripts. Others simply assumed the transition without showing any variation in note size. We found in any embellished song we selected that diminutive notes did not always precede the long or main note; sometimes they followed the main note, as in the second measure of staff six of "Simple Gifts."

The first embellishment inserted in "Simple Gifts" in this section is a shake or quaver (trill). It is short, not emphasized, and has a micropitch change in tone that is not quite a semitone. Time is borrowed from the long note and given to the diminutive note. The upturns indicated by the asterisks are late and emphasized. This practice enables the dancer to take short smooth steps to the main note that follows rather than making an abrupt leap to it. In singing, one ought to start the word or syllable on the diminutive note preceding the main note.

In practice, this slide was often less than graceful. Sliding or whooping up to a note by inserting a grace note on the way was common in Protestant camp meeting songs during the pre–Civil War revival period as well as in secular British and American folk songs. Anyone familiar with traditional folk singers in the mountain coves, lumberjack camps, and small towns of Appalachia should be well acquainted with the "whooping" phenomenon.

We have added embellishment notations to the "Simple Gifts" song in this section to demonstrate how Brother Ricardo sang it. When using the "whoop," he began singing the text word or syllable that immediately followed the "whoop" symbol at the point where the "whoop" symbol appears. In listening to him, we heard a very pronounced detachment immediately after each of the two staccato notes. Brother Ricardo's abrupt endings of phrases and verses reflected the Shaker belief that dragging out the last words of a song was ostentatious and contrary to the Shaker belief in simplicity.[18] Each rest in this version of "Simple Gifts" is a red flag signaling that there is a very abrupt ending to the note preceding the rest.

Square Order Shuffle Dance Instructions

The Square Order Shuffle is probably the oldest organized or structured Shaker dance (fig. 25). In teaching this dance to teenagers at Shaker Village, Brother Ricardo paired it with "Simple Gifts." He showed how the Shakers arranged themselves in solid squares—a "square" of women facing a "square" of men with a suitable distance between them. For example, if there were twenty-five women and twenty-five men, each square embraced five horizontal rows and five vertical rows. Whatever the number, the intent was to arrange the dancers in as true a square formation as possible. When the Shakers found that the dance area did not accommodate square formations, they then adapted to rectangular formations.

Some Shaker manuscripts and published song collections repeat both sections of "Simple Gifts," as in the case of D 67, "'Tis the gift to be simple." Other collections do not repeat either section; neither did Brother Ricardo. He instructed the singers to stand to one side, to sing the song throughout without repeating any part of it, and to keep in sync with the dancers. Diagram instructions A and B, repeated four times, describe the dance pattern for the first section of the song; likewise, instructions A and C, repeated four times, describe the dance pattern for the second section of the song. Dancers may dance through this pattern as often as necessary for the occasion at hand.

The "tip tap" indicated in figure #25 refers to foot action only and is not vocalized. Because the foot action for the "tip tap" in box C does not work out to a full ninety-degree turn, dancers must complete the turn while stepping into the next beat of the forward movement, as shown in box A. Footprint 4 in box A and 9 in boxes B and C show that only the toes

Brother Ricardo's Square Order Shuffle

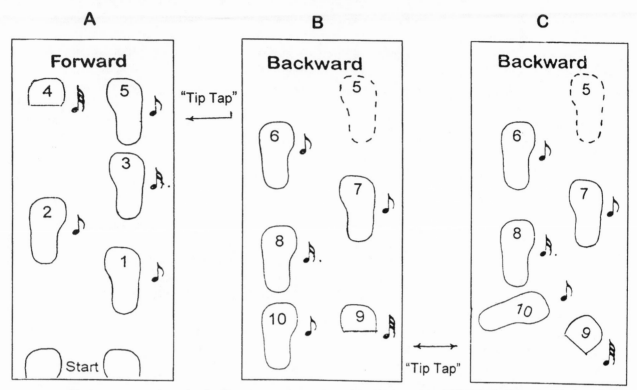

Sequence: A & B four times, then A & C four times.

Fig. 25. The Square Order Shuffle as remembered by Brother Ricardo Belden. Design by Stu Jamieson. COMPUTER GRAPHIC BY DEAHNARA KNAUTH REGAN AND STEVE SHERMAN.

make contact with the floor. The foot makes full heel-to-toe contact with the floor for all other foot action.[19]

Circle Dance Instructions

Brother Ricardo's version of "Who will bow and bend" varies from the version in manuscript C. For example, he sang "flowing" instead of "blowing" and repeated the second part of the song. According to his instructions, dance participants match their action with the words sung by a group of singers standing to the side (fig. 26). The dancers form a double circle. One half of each circle has all men; the other half, all women. The double circle means that men are paired with men, and women with women. A "traveling gender gap" always remains during the dance. The dancers face right, proceed in a counterclockwise direction, and match action to the words:

"Who will *bow* . . ." While stepping ahead, make a modi-

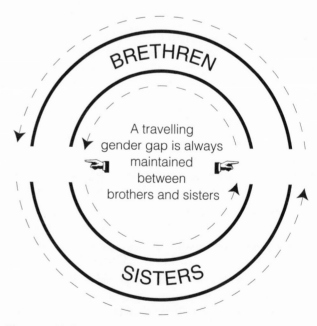

Fig. 26. A Circle Dance as remembered by Brother Ricardo Belden. GRAPHIC BY STEVE SHERMAN.

Who will bow and bend like a willow

Sung by Brother Ricardo Belden
at Shaker Village, New Lebanon, N. Y.

Briskly (♩ =108)

Who will bow and bend like a wil - low? Who will turn and

twist and reel In the gale of sim - ple free- dom

From the bower of un - ion blow- ing? Who will drink the

wine of pow - er Drop- ping down like a show - er?

Pride and bond - age all for - get - ing, Moth- er's wine is

free - ly work- ing. Oh! Ho! I will have it,

I will bow and bend to get it; I'll be reel - ing,

turn - ing. twist- ing; Shake out all the starch and stiff- 'ning.

fied "gathering of blessings" gesture, that is, a deep bow, the upper body not quite to the horizontal position, with arms spread sideways and down in a 45-degree angle and slightly back; palms cupped upward. Emphasis is on the upward sweep.

"...and *bend* like a willow?" Come up from bow, and even before body is upright, begin to turn and twist on heels.

"Who will *turn* and *twist* and *reel*..." Continue turning on heels in rhythm; each individual makes a full turn, or perhaps two turns.

"... in the gale of simple freedom from the bower of union blowing?" Use the "gathering of blessings" gesture.

"Who will *drink* the wine of power..." Use the "gathering of blessings" gesture but with palms cupped upward, pinkies touching, and heels of palms touching. This gesture mimes that of a person scooping up water from a water basin in order to quench thirst. This is a hand gesture, not a bending-at-the-waist gesture. The emphasis is on the upward sweep to chin level while the dancer is still advancing.

"... *Dropping* down like a *shower*?" Using an undulating movement with palms vertical, held apart about nine inches, and facing each other, move hands downward to waist height.

"Pride and bondage all forgetting, Mother's wine is freely working. (CHORUS) Oh! Ho! I will have it. I will bend bow and bend to get it. I'll be reeling, turning, twisting, ..." Repeat the instructions for the first three motions: "Who will bow... and bend like a willow... Who will turn and twist and reel..."

"... *Shake* out all the starch and stiff'ning." Now halt and shake. The men stand in place with backs strongly arched backwards, heads tilted back, and faces upward; clenched fists are out at the side at a 45-degree angle, and arms are vibrating. Both heels, one in synchronization with the other, are heavily thudded on the floor. Each male is not necessarily in synchronization with other males or with the beat. Think of rolling thunder! Women, using the same body posture and hand motion, quiver their lower limbs instead of thudding their heels on the floor.

In this very gesture-oriented dance, the words control the gestures, and the two are synchronized as much as possible. The participants march throughout the dance, except when they stop to perform the shaking motion explained in the last step of the instructions.

Appendix A: Shaker and Community Names in the Song Manuscripts

The Shaker scribes affixed the names listed below to some of the songs we selected from the manuscripts. Many songs we selected have no such credit assigned. The numbers indicate song numbers, not page numbers.

A. W. (Anna White?), 112
Barrett, Andrew, 56, 60, 61, 62, 69n
Brackett, William C., 16n
Clark, Elder (George), 59
DeWitt, Henry, 13, 14n, 15
Doolittle, Julia, 14
Doolittle, Maryan (Antoinette), 14
Eades, H(arvey) L., 25
Eades, I. R., 7
Fairbanks, Oliver, 5
Fairchild, C. M., 95
H. G. (Harriet Gill?), 34
Harrison, Keturah, 8
Hollister, Henry, 81

I. L. J., 78
Mason, Sarah, 49n
McLean, Myra, 57
M. J. A., 108
M. R., 113
Perkins, Abraham, 2, 16
Perkins, William H., 117
Smith, Benjamin, 73n
Smith, Eldress Betsy, 66
Smith, Jane, 4
Wells, N. (Nancy?), 9
Whicher, Eldress Mary, 52
(Whitaker), Father James, 19
Youngs, Isaac N., 1, 3, 11, 18, 20n

Names of Shaker communities were sometimes appended to the songs selected from the original manuscripts. They are listed in order of frequency of appearance. Fewer than half of the songs selected have site identification.

New Lebanon, New York: 17. Three of these songs bear the site designation "Mount Lebanon" which was the name for New Lebanon as of 1861.
South Union, Kentucky: 12
Watervliet, New York: 6
Enfield, New Hampshire: 6. Three of these songs bear the site designation "North Enfield." North Enfield was a distance from the Enfield Shaker site but, with the coming of a railroad, the Enfield Church Family established weaving mills, saw mills, and other businesses there during the 1840s.

Harvard, Massachusetts: 4
Canterbury, New Hampshire: 3
Enfield, Connecticut: 2
Canaan, New York: 1
Hancock Church, Massachusetts: 1
H. Mt. (?): 1
Olive Branch, Florida: 1
Pleasant Hill, Kentucky: 1
Whitewater, Ohio: 1

Appendix B: Haskell's Cursive Notation

As evident in Manuscript F, Russel Haskell's cursive letteral notation consists of a single line of symbolic notes written below the appropriate words.[1] Conversion to conventional notation is not difficult, though not necessarily immediately obvious.

The songs were written on lined pages; these lines help identify the intended octave. Every note has a unique symbol within an octave range. Notes related by an octave are shown by the relative positioning of the notes around a casual reference line.

All songs are in G major or in D minor. Singers may need to transpose an occasional song to a higher or lower key to suit their voices.

Note duration is changed by (1) an added dot to indicate one and one-half times the original value; (2) a vertical bar to indicate a doubling of the original values; (3) a dash above or below the note to indicate one-half the original value; (4) a double or triple dash above the note to indicate one-fourth or one-eighth of the original value; (5) a slur across several notes to show that the effective duration is the sum of both of the original notes; and (6) a combination of these notations. The notes without any dots or dashes should be considered quarter notes.

The rhythm and tempo are indicated at the beginning of the song by a fraction, a small number, and/or a symbol. The prefixed fraction written in many of the Shaker songs is *not* a time signature as in conventional notation.

Each song is in one of two classes: (1) an even number of notes per unit, as in the conventional 2/4, 4/4 time; or (2) an odd number of notes per beat, as in the conventional 3/8 or 6/8 time. The rhythm and tempo indications at the beginning of each song were intended to help the Shakers who could read music to interpret rhythm and tempo.

The songs are rarely divided into measures; therefore, the transcriber must decide which meter to use.

A procedure for transcribing into standard notation follows.

1. Write the words below the staff.
2. Assume initially that the song is written in either 4/4 or 6/8 time.
3. Translate the symbolic notes into conventional staff notation. A note with no time adjustment (i.e., no added dots or associated vertical bars) is a quarter note.
4. Assign appropriate bar lines to indicate measures. Sing the song to aid in finding the natural pulse that appears in key places in the song. Calculating the full measures forward and backward from these key notes may help to make pickup notes more obvious.
5. Place repeat signs in the proper places. Usually, the song is in two parts. Each part is sung twice in succession and the total song is repeated as often as desired.
6. The beginning and ending measures in each part sometimes need adjustment in order to have the correct number of beats in each measure.
7. Prefix a correct time signature and the key notation.
8. The song may be in an awkward key; if so, transpose it to a convenient relative key.

Appendix C: A Hancock Shaker Recollection

This account highlights memories of a childhood glimpse into aspects of life at the Hancock Shaker community during the same decade (1942–1952) in which Brother Ricardo Belden gave the song manuscripts to Jerome Count.[1]

Ila Hanson Mongillo, a former student with whom we still have contact, grew up in New Lebanon, New York, and has special memories of the time her mother, Ruby Hanson, performed household tasks for the Hancock Shakers two days a week between 1942 and 1947. She often accompanied her mother to the Shaker community on days when her school was not in session.

At that time there were very few Shakers left at Hancock. Even though their membership was too small to require the use of all of their buildings, they still maintained small vegetable and flower gardens and kept a few cows and chickens. The declining membership, combined with advancing age, forced the Shakers to hire help from outside their community. Ila believes that Frieda Sipple and Adeline Pattison were the youngest of the Shaker sisters. Other Shakers with whom Ila and her mother had ongoing contact were Eldress Fannie Estabrook, Brother Ricardo Belden, and his sister, Elizabeth Belden. Frances Hall, a trustee, worked and lived not in the dwelling house but in the white house reserved for trustees. She handled business arrangements and served as the liaison with the outside community. Ila also has a vague memory of Sadie Neal, who had died shortly after her transfer from New Lebanon in 1947.

Ila remembers that the Shakers at Hancock all lived and had their meals in the brick dwelling house that faces Route 20, a main highway that runs through New York State and Massachusetts. As a little girl, she felt very small sitting in the large dining room with only a few people eating at two of the tables. Ila, her mother, and the Shaker sisters sat at a table near the dumbwaiter, while Brother Ricardo sat alone at the other end of the room. The cook, who worked below in the kitchen, was hired from the outside.

One of Ila's warmest memories of the Shaker sisters is how fun-loving they were. She says that they displayed a keen sense of humor and often played little jokes on one another. Ila recalls that she often heard sisters humming or singing to themselves when they were in their rooms but that she never heard them singing together.

Ila remembers that Brother Ricardo was often at a loss as to how to converse with a child—and a girl child at that! When she wandered around the dwelling house, she often found Brother Ricardo at work in his clock shop. It was there that he showed and explained clock mechanisms to Ila, who still has the clock that her mother purchased from him in the 1940s. Brother Ricardo was always courteous to her, but she recognized even then that he was relieved when she returned to the company of the sisters. Ila still glows with the memory of how special she felt, because the Shaker sisters loved having a child on the site and beamed with pleasure whenever she visited them.

Notes

Preface (pp. xvii–xx)

1. Edward D. Andrews, *The Gift to Be Simple: Songs, Dances, and Rituals of the American Shakers* (New York: J. J. Augustin, 1940; reprint, New York: Dover Publications, 1962; copyright renewed by Faith Andrews, 1967).
2. Daniel W. Patterson, *The Shaker Spiritual* (Princeton: Princeton University Press, 1979; 2nd, corrected ed., New York: Dover Publications, 2000).
3. Patterson, *The Shaker Spiritual,* 2nd, corrected ed., 2000, xxiv.
4. Harold E. Cook, *Shaker Music: A Manifestation of American Folk Culture* (Lewisburg, Pa.: Bucknell University Press; Cranbury, N.J.: Associated University Presses, 1973).
5. Stephen J. Stein, *The Shaker Experience in America* (New Haven: Yale University Press, 1992), 300.
6. "Shaker Music Lives Again," *Berkshire Sketch,* 14 August 1952, 4–5, 9–13.
7. *Fourteen Shaker Songs Teenage Chorus,* with an introduction by Shaker Brother Ricardo Belden and Jerome Count (Mt. Lebanon, N.Y.: Shaker Village Work Group, 1957), LP TV 25548–Side 1.
8. Ibid.
9. Sybil Count, conversation with authors, New Lebanon, N.Y., 7 April 1995.
10. Stu Jamieson, telephone conversation with authors, 23 September 1989.
11. Russel Haskell, Enfield, Conn., letter to Isaac N. Youngs, New Lebanon, N.Y., 10 February 1834, Western Reserve Historical Society Library, Cleveland, Shaker Collection, mss. IV–A–9.
12. Andrew Houston, Union Village, Ohio, letter to Isaac N. Youngs, New Lebanon, N.Y., 16 October 1841, Western Reserve Historical Society Library, Cleveland, Shaker Collection, mss. IV: A–72.
13. John A. Lomax and Alan Lomax, *American Ballads and Folk Songs* (New York: MacMillan, 1934), xxxv.
14. Charles Seeger and Ruth Seeger, musical foreword to John Lomax and Alan Lomax *Best Loved American Folk Songs,* (New York: Grossett and Dunlap, 1947), xii.
15. Thomas Brown, *An Account of the People Called Shakers: Their Faith, Doctrine and Practice* (1812; reprint, New York: AMS, 1977), 143–145.
16. Patterson, *The Shaker Spiritual,* 2nd, corrected ed., 2000, xviii–xx.

Notes on Transcribing and Editing (p. xxvii)

1. Cook, *Shaker Music,* 7–8.

1. Manuscript A (pp. 1–5)

1. Isaac N. Youngs, *A Short Abridgement of the Rules of Music with Lessons for Exercise and a Few Observations for New Beginners* (New Lebanon, N.Y., 1843), Russel Haskell, *A Manual Expositor: Or, A Treatise on the Rules and Elements of Music* (New York: James W. Wood, 1847).
2. Patterson, *The Shaker Spiritual,* 2nd, corrected ed., 2000, 517.
3. Ibid., 43.
4. Ibid.
5. *Fourteen Shaker Songs,* LP TV 25548–Side 1.
6. Julia Neal, *The Kentucky Shakers* (Lexington: University Press of Kentucky, 1962), 93–94; Stein, *The Shaker Experience,* 255–256.
7. Tommy Hines, e-mail to authors, 31 January 2002.

2. Manuscript B (p. 76)

1. David R. Lamson, *Two Years Experience Among the Shakers* (West Boylston, Mass., 1848), 56–57.
2. Ibid., 57–58.
3. Ibid., 62–67.

3. Manuscript C (p. 82)

1. Patterson, *The Shaker Spiritual,* 2nd, corrected ed., 2000, 480.
2. Cook, *Shaker Music,* 251.
3. Roger Hall, comp. and ed., *A Guide to Shaker Music: With Music Supplement* (Stoughton, Mass.: Pinetree Press, 1997), 11.
4. Andrews, *The Gift to Be Simple,* 123.

4. Manuscript D (p. 120)

1. Cook, *Shaker Music*, 291.
2. Aaron Copland, *Appalachian Spring: Ballet for Martha* [full score], New York: Boosey & Hawkes, 1945; also *Appalachian Spring: Ballet for Martha: Suite Version for Thirteen Instruments* (New York: Boosey & Hawkes, 1971).
3. Nancy Langstaff and John Langstaff, *The Christmas Revels Songbook*, 2nd ed. (Cambridge: Revels Inc., 1995), 46–47; Carlton Young, ed., Revision Committee. *United Methodist Hymnal* (Nashville: United Methodist Publishing House, 1989), 261–262.

Manuscript E (p. 152)

1. Rev. David MacRae, *The Americans at Home: Pen and Ink Sketches of American Men, Manners, and Institutions*, vol. 1 (Glasgow: John Smith & Son, 1870, 1908), 336.
2. Ibid., 338.
3. Ibid., 339.

6. Manuscript F (pp. 180–181)

1. Patterson, *The Shaker Spiritual*, 47.
2. Haskell, *A Manual Expositor*, 61.
3. Youngs, *A Short Abridgement*, 17.

7. Manuscript G (pp. 232–233)

1. Viola E. Woodruff Opdahl, "William Pillow: His Life among the Shakers," *The Yorker* (November–December 1956), 26.
2. Carol Weisbrod, *The Boundaries of Utopia* (New York: Pantheon Books, 1980), 57.
3. V. Opdahl, "William Pillow," 27.

8. Manuscript H (p. 242)

1. *Fourteen Shaker Songs*, LP TV 25548—Side 1.

9. Manuscript I (p. 254)

1. William Cullen Bryant, "Death of Lincoln," in *English Poetry: From Tennyson to Whitman*, vol. 42, bk. 3, *The Harvard Classics*, ed. Charles W. Elliot (New York: P.F. Collier, 1963), 1223–1224.

10. Beyond the Manuscripts (pp. 268–280)

1. S. Count, conversation with authors, New Lebanon, N.Y., 7 April 1995.
2. V. Opdahl, "William Pillow," 26.
3. Gloria Jamieson, telephone conversation with authors, 13 August 2001.
4. *Fourteen Shaker Songs*, LP TV 25548—Side 1.
5. Andrews, *The Gift to Be Simple*, 118.
6. Barbara Pickhardt, Artistic Director, and the Hudson Valley Youth Chorale, *The Magic of Music* concert, 13 and 14 May 2001.
7. Patterson, *The Shaker Spiritual*, 383.
8. Andrews, *The Gift to Be Simple*, 126; Patterson, *The Shaker Spiritual*, 363.
9. Patterson, letter to authors, January 2003.
10. Stu Jamieson, e-mails to authors, 28 June 2001, 16 April 2002.
11. Derobigne M. Bennett and Isaac N. Youngs, *Journal of Inspired Meetings*, 1 November 1840, Western Reserve Historical Society Library, Cleveland: Shaker Collection, ms VIII B-138.
12. Stu Jamieson, letter to authors, 25 January 2001.
13. Stu Jamieson, e-mail to authors, 28 June 2001.
14. Jacqui McDonald, conversation with authors, Hurley, N.Y., 24 October 2001, 20 October 2002.
15. Evelyn Kendrick Wells, *The Ballad Tree* (New York: The Ronald Press Co., 1950), 197.
16. Percy R. Dearmer, Vaughn Williams, and Martin Shaw, *The Oxford Book of Carols* (London: Oxford University Press, 1928), 154–155.
17. Youngs, *A Short Abridgement*, 7, 26.
18. Stu Jamieson, letters to authors, 11 June 1994, 25 January 2001.
19. Stu Jamieson, telephone conversation with authors, 2 July 2001; letters to authors, 25 January 2001, 16 April 2002.

Appendix B (p. 285)

1. The source for the following is Robert C. Opdahl, "Shaker Symbolic Music," rev. (New Lebanon: Shaker Village Work Camp, 1953), 1–3, 5.

Appendix C (p. 287)

1. Ila Hanson Mongillo, interview by authors, Hurley, N.Y., 3 January 2003.

Song Notes

1. Manuscript A

4. *"Let music sound and echo 'round."* The reference to playing on harps is symbolic. Shakers frowned on the use of musical instruments until late in the nineteenth century.

6. *"I am determined to be free."* The notes in the first half of the second part of the edited version are raised an octave higher than those in the original manuscript. This change is intended to make the song more singable.

8. *"I will labor to be free."* The Shaker scribe separated measures with blank spaces instead of bars, hence, the spaces in the transcript version of this song. We chose to eliminate the "for" that precedes "simplicity" in the edited version because we felt that "love" in the first staff should be on a strong beat.

10. *"I will be free, I'll not be bound."* The unknown Shaker who composed this song made it very clear that he needed help to fight a personal battle against haughtiness and wickedness. Any Shaker adhering strictly to Shaker beliefs would have understood the spiritual significance of this struggle against vanity and evil.

13. *"In this new and living way."* The Shaker scribe or composer assigned only two notes to the three-syllable "heavenly" in the first measure of the second staff.

14. *"May we now in pure devotion."* The Shaker scribed omitted the "g" in *Kingdom* in the last staff of the manuscript.

16. *"O freedom, lovely in my eyes."* This is the only song in our collection in which the scribe used shape notes. See the introduction to section one for details.

19. *"Farewell unto this world."* Father James Whitaker, who came to this country in 1774 with Mother Ann Lee, wrote this song. Although he survived his trip from England by only thirteen years, he was a significant instrument in shaping the subsequent course of the Shaker movement.

21. *"Little Big I."* The dramatic plea for help in the struggle against feelings or displays of self-importance and vanity echoes the same request found in A 10, "I will be free I'll not be bound."

26. *"Shout, shout, shout and sing."* This is the first song in Manuscript A that is dated 1848, all of the preceding dated songs read 1835. The small letteral notation used here has no trace of Eades's linear notation style.

30. *"A Laughing Song."* Edward Andrews on page 121 of his book *"The Gift to Be Simple"* titled this song "Black Bill's Wonderment." He identified its provenance as Canterbury and dated it February 22, 1847.

34. *"Like a little busy bee."* There is a double note in the third staff of the transcript copy. We eliminated the lower of the two notes in the edited version.

3. Manuscript C

38. *"(Lodle lo lodle lodle lodle lo)."* This song, and E 73, "(Lodle lo lodle lodle lo)," have no titles or text in their manuscript formats. We have used vocables for both text and titles and have enclosed the titles in parentheses.

42. *"Hear Mother Calling."* The text phrase lacks a note for "it is afalling." To compensate for its absence, we split an eighth note into two sixteenth notes.

46. *"Bonny Wee One."* The difficulty encountered in translating some of the dialect words is detailed in the introduction to section three.

48. *"Who will bow and bend like a willow."* This song, with variations, is paired with dance instructions in the last section of this book.

49. *"I feel the gentle breezes blow."* The inscription added to this song in the original manuscript—"Given by Sarah Mason, a colored sister, on the evening of her Decease"—provides a poignant example of the gift of song among the Shakers even during their last moments.

54. *"Sweet Afton."* Here, the Shaker composer used the easily recognized tune found in Martin Luther's "Cradle Hymn" and Robert Burn's "Flow Gently Sweet Afton." It is a very easily recognized example of the Shakers borrowing familiar tunes and putting their own words to them.

4. Manuscript D

57. *"Sowing the seed of the Springtime."* Most of the songs that we have selected contain repeat signs for either both parts of a song

291

or for only the second part. In this instance, the scribe inserted a repeat sign for only the first part.

5. Manuscript E

70. *"Shuffling Tune."* The text leaves no doubt as to the nature of the dance to be performed with this song.
80. *"Whither, O whither on earth can I roam."* This two-versed hymn is an unapologetic paean to Shaker life. One wonders how many backsliding members this song might have helped stay within the fold.

6. Manuscript F

87. *"With joy we chant."* The Shakers welcomed newcomers with special songs such as this very buoyant and joyous example.
98. *"Not one sparrow is forgotten."* This song is also in the Shaker hymnal *Shaker Music: Original Inspirational Hymns and Songs Illustrative of the Resurrection Life and Testimony of the Shakers.* (1884; reprint, Sabbathday Lake, Maine: The Shaker Press, n.d.), 97.
102. *"To the land of the blest."* This is the only song in Manuscript F in which Haskell inserted measure bars.

103. *"Send, O Lord, thy holy power."* The composer of this two-versed hymn, like those who wrote A 10, "I will be free I'll not be bound," and A 21, "Little Big I," asked for haughtiness to be struck down.
106. *"Mov'd by the spirit of the Lord."* Does the reference to the "narrow path" here reflect the traditional concept of a narrow path that transcends a number of religious groups, or is it echoing the foot movement for "Precept on Precept" described in section ten?

7. Manuscript G

109. *"Love me, bless me, holy angels."* The Shaker copyist wrote a double note in the first measure of the fifth staff.
110. *"I'm glad I am a Shaker."* The placement of the apostrophes in the manuscript copy of this song is unique!

9. Manuscript I

119. *"Farewell Song."* Farewell lacks one "l" throughout the manuscript copy.

Glossary

alway. Archaic form of *always.*
bond. A poetic reference to enslaved people.
brethern. Old variant of *brethren.*
buisy. Obsolete form of *busy.*
dews. A misspelling of *dew.*
farewel. Old form of *farewell.*
laught. Old variant of *laugh.*
moulding. Old variant of *molding.*

relmes. A misspelling of *realms.*
Selan. A heavenly spirit.
sercher. Obsolete form of *searcher.*
togeather. Old variant of *together.*
valiently. Rare, obsolete form of *valiantly.*
withe. A flexible twig.
wordy. Obsolete form of *worldly.*

Works Cited

Andrews, Edward D. *The Gift to Be Simple: Songs, Dances and Rituals of the American Shakers*. New York: J. J. Augustin Publisher, 1940; reprint, New York: Dover Publications, 1962; copyright renewed by Faith Andrews, 1967.

Bennett, Derobigne M., and Isaac N. Youngs. *Journal of Inspired Meetings*. 1 November 1840. Western Reserve Historical Society Library, Cleveland Shaker Collection, ms VIII B-138.

Brown, Thomas. *An Account of the People Called Shakers: Their Faith, Doctrines, and Practice*. 1812; reprint, New York: AMS, 1977.

Bryant, William Cullen. "Death of Lincoln," in *English Poetry from Tennyson to Whitman*, vol. 42, bk. 3. *The Harvard Classics*, ed. Charles W. Elliot. New York: P. F. Collier & Sons Corp., 1963.

Cook, Harold E. *Shaker Music: A Manifestation of American Folk Culture*. Lewisburg: Bucknell University Press; Cranberry, N.J.: Associated University Presses, 1973.

Copland, Aaron. *Appalachian Spring: Ballet for Martha* [full score]. New York: Boosey & Hawkes, 1945.

———. *Appalachian Spring: Ballet for Martha: Suite Version for Thirteen Instruments*. New York: Boosey & Hawkes, 1971.

Dearmer, Percy, R. Vaughn Williams, and Martin Shaw. *The Oxford Book of. Carols*. London: Oxford University Press, 1928.

Fourteen Shaker Songs. Teenage chorus, with an introduction by Shaker Brother Belden and Jerome Count. Mt. Lebanon, N.Y.: Shaker Village Work Group, 1957, LP TV 25548 - side 1.

Hall, Roger, comp. and ed. *A Guide to Shaker Music: With Music Supplement*. Stoughton, Mass.: Pinetree Press, 1997.

Haskell, Russel. Letter to Isaac N. Youngs, New Lebanon, N.Y., 10 February 1834. Western Reserve Historical Society Library, Cleveland Shaker Collection, ms. IV: A-9.

———. *A Manual Expositor: Or A Treatise on the Rules and Elements of Music*. New York: James Wood, 1847.

Houston, Andrew. Letter to Isaac N. Youngs, New Lebanon, N.Y., 16 October 1841. Western Reserve Historical Society Library, Cleveland Shaker Collection, ms. IV: A-72.

Jackson, George Pullen. *White Spirituals in the Southern Uplands*. Chapel Hill: University of North Carolina Press, 1933; reprint, New York: Dover Publications, 1965.

Lamson, David R. *Two Years Experience among the Shakers*. West Boylston, Mass., 1848.

Langstaff, Nancy, and John Langstaff. *The Christmas Revels Songbook*, 2nd ed. Cambridge: Revels, Inc., 1995.

Lomax, John A., and Alan Lomax. *American Ballads and Folk Songs*. New York: MacMillan, 1934.

MacRae, Rev. David. *The Americans at Home: Pen and Ink Sketches of American Men, Manners, and Institutions*, vol. 1. Glasgow: John Smith & Son, 1870, 1908.

Neal, Julia. *The Kentucky Shakers*. Lexington: University Press of Kentucky, 1962.

Opdahl, Viola E. Woodruff. "William Pillow: His Life among the Shakers," *The Yorker* #15 (November–December 1956) 23–27.

Patterson, Daniel W. *The Shaker Spiritual*. Princeton, N.J.: Princeton University Press, 1979; 2nd, corrected ed., New York: Dover Publications, 2000.

Seeger, Charles, and Ruth Seeger. Musical foreword to *Best Loved American Folk Songs*, by John and Alan Lomax. New York: Grossett and Dunlap, 1947.

"Shaker Music Lives Again." *Berkshire Sketch*, 14 August 1952, 4–5, 9–13.

Stein, Stephen J. *The Shaker Experience in America*. New Haven: Yale University Press, 1992.

Weisbrod, Carol. *The Boundaries of Utopia*. New York: Pantheon Books, 1980.

Wells, Evelyn Kendrick. *The Ballad Tree*. New York: The Ronald Press Company, 1950.

Young, Carlton, ed., revision committee, *United Methodist Hymnal*. Nashville: United Methodist Publishing House, 1989.

Youngs, Isaac N. *A Short Abridgement of the Rules of Music with Lessons for Exercise and a Few Observations for New Beginners*. New Lebanon, N.Y., 1843.

Works Consulted

Works Published by or for the Shakers

1. General History

The Manifesto, vols. 1–29. Canterbury, N.H.: The United Societies (Shaker Village), 1871–1899. (Published on the first of each month, with notes about music; titles varied.)

Youngs, Benjamin S., and Calvin Green. *Testimony of Christ's First and Second Appearing, Exemplified by the Principles and Practices of the True Church of Christ,* 4th ed. Albany, N.Y.: Published by the Shakers, Van Benthusen Press, 1856. (Darrow, David, John Meacham, and Benjamin S. Youngs, 1st ed., 1808.)

2. Music

A Collection of Hymns and Anthems Adapted to Public Worship. (Cover title: *Hymns and Anthems for the Hour of Worship.*) East Canterbury, N.H.: The Shakers, 1892.

Original Shaker Music Published by the North Family of Mt. Lebanon, Col. Co., N.Y., vol. 2. (Cover title: *Original Shaker Music, Volume II.*) 1893. (Reprint, Sabbathday Lake, Me.: The Shaker Press, n.d.)

Phelps, Lillian. *Shaker Music: A Brief History.* Canterbury, N.H.: Nazer, 1964.

Philos Harmoniae (Ricard McNemar). *A Selection of Hymns and Poems for the Use of Believers: Collected from Sundry Authors.* Watervliet, Ohio, 1833.

Shaker Music: Inspirational Hymns and Melodies Illustrative of the Resurrection, Life, and Testimony of the Shakers. (Cover title: *Shaker Music*). 1875. (Reprint, New York: AMS, 1974.)

Shaker Music: Inspirational Hymns and Songs Illustrative of the Resurrection, Life, and Testimony of the Shakers. (Cover title: *Original Inspirational Shaker Music*). Published for the North Family, New Lebanon, N.Y., 1884, copyright by Daniel Orford. (Reprint, Sabbathday Lake, Me.: United Society of Shakers, n.d.)

Works Published by Others

1. General History

Andrews, Edward D. *The People Called Shakers.* New York: Oxford University Press, 1953.

Campion, Nardi Reeder. *Mother Ann Lee: Moving Star of the Shakers.* Hanover, N.H.: University Press of New England, 1990. (Published in 1976 as *Ann the Word.*)

Count, Jerome. "The Shakers." *Berkshire Sketch* (26 June 1952), 4–5.

———. "The Shakers: An American Phenomenon." *Design* (Spring 1952), 60–65.

Melcher, Marguerite Fellows. *The Shaker Adventure.* Princeton, N.J.: Princeton University Press, 1941.

Van Kolken, Dianna. *Introducing the Shakers: An Explanation and Directory.* Bowling Green, Ohio: Gabriel's Horn, 1985.

2. Music

Collins, Mitzi, and Colleen Liggett, compilers. *Joy of Angels: Shaker Spirituals for Christmas and the New Year.* Rochester, N.Y.: Sampler Records, 1995.

Druckman, Jacob, arranger. *The Simple Gifts: A Cantata Based on Themes of the American Shakers.* Dedicated to the Shaker Village Work Group. Copyright by Jacob Druckman, 1954.

Goodwillie, Christian, compiler and editor. *Shaker Songs: A Celebration of Peace, Harmony, and Simplicity.* With contributions from Joel Cohen. New York: Black Dog and Leventhal, 2002.

Grant, Jerry V. *Shaker, Noble but Plain: The Shaker Meeting House at Mount Lebanon.* Old Chatham, N.Y.: The Shaker Museum and Library, 1994.

Hall, Roger, compiler and editor. *Love Is a Little: A Sampling of Shaker Spirituals.* Rochester, N.Y.: Sampler Records, 1996.

Held, Conrad. *Fifteen Shaker Songs.* New York: G. Schirmer, 1944.

Mahoney, Kathleen. *Simple Wisdom: Shaker Sayings, Poems and Songs.* New York: Viking Penguin, 1993.

Patterson, Daniel. *Nine Shaker Spirituals (With a Brief Account of Early Shaker Song).* Old Chatham, N.Y.: The Shaker Museum Foundation, 1964.

Rich, Gail. *Simple Gifts Songs.* Pacific, Mo.: Mel Bay, 1994.

"Shaker Music Lives Again." *Berkshire Sketch* (14 August 1952), 4–5.

Sturm, Ann Black, compiler. *The Shaker Gift of Song: A Book of Shaker Songs.* Frankfurt, Ky.: Berea College Press, 1981.

Wertkin, Gerard C. *The Four Seasons of Shaker Life: An Intimate Portrait of The Community at Sabbathday Lake, Maine.* New York: Simon and Schuster, 1986.

3. For Children

Moriarty, Kathleen M. *A Shaker Sampler Coloring Book.* Poland Springs, Maine: The United Society of Shakers, Sabbathday Lake, 1990.

Ray, Mary Lyn. *Angel Baskets: A Little Story About the Shakers.* Sanbornton, N.H.: Martha Wetherbee Books, 1987.

———. *Shaker Boy.* San Diego: Browndeer/Harcourt Brace, 1994.

Thorne-Thomsen, Kathleen. *Shaker Children: True Stories and Crafts.* Chicago: Chicago Review, 1996. (Includes information on songs and dances.)

4. Shaker Village Work Education Foundation, Inc. (Shaker Village Work Camp)

Songs of the Shakers. Mt. Lebanon, N.Y.: Shaker Village Work Group, 1956.

Songs of the Shakers. Mt. Lebanon, N.Y.: Work Education Foundation, Inc., 1962.

"Visiting the Shakers in 1857." *Harper's New Monthly Magazine* (1857): 165–171. (Reprint, Mt. Lebanon, N.Y.: Shaker Village Work Camp, n.d).

Wickersham, George M. *How I Came to Be A Shaker.* 1891. (Reprint, Mt. Lebanon, N.Y.: Shaker Village Work Camp, n.d.).

Audio Recordings

Early Shaker Spirituals. Sung by Sister R. Mildred Barker and Other Members of the United Society of Shakers, Sabbathday Lake, Maine. Notes by Daniel E. Patterson. Cassette 0078. Somerville, Ma.: Rounder, 1976.

Folger, Randy, composer, editor, and performer. *Gentle Words.* Cassette, CD. Pleasant Hill, Ky.: American Productions, 1993.

Folger, Randy, Colleen Liggett, Kathy Leigh Johnson, Mitzi Collins, et al. *The Joy of Angels: Shaker Spirituals for Christmas and the New Year.* Cassette, CD 9628. Rochester, N.Y.: Sampler Records, 1995.

Haagen, Mary Ann, Carolyn Smith, and Ronald Boehm, producers, with the Singers of Lower Shaker Village (Mary Ann Haagen, director). *All at Home—34 Gift Songs, Hymns, and Anthems,* Cassette, CD. Enfield, N.H.: Museum of Lower Shaker Village and Impact Media, 1995.

Hall, Roger L,. composer and editor, and Mitzi Collins. *Love Is a Little: A Sampling of Shaker Spirituals.* 2nd ed. Cassette, CD. Rochester, N.Y.: Sampler Records, 1992.

O Hear Their Music Ring: 35 Songs of the Shakers. The Singers of Lower Shaker Village, Mary Ann Wilde, producer. Cassette. Enfield, N.H.: Museum of Lower Shaker Village, 1989.

Opdahl, Robert C., composer and editor, with the Woodstock Singers. *Selected Songs of the Shakers.* Cassette. Shokan, N.Y., 1970.

Simple Gifts and Other Songs. The Berkshire Consort. LP (7 inch EP, 33 1/3 RPM AH740118-A; 4024- 9A, A-H41018- B; 4024-9B). N.p.: Audio Heritage, [197_].

Simple Gifts: Shaker Chants and Spirituals, Shakers of Sabbathday Lake. The Boston Camerata, Joel Cohen, music director, the Schola Cantorum of Boston, Frederick Jodry, director, and the Shaker Community of Sabbathday Lake, Maine. Cassette. 1995.

Randle, William, editor. *The Shaker Heritage.* The Shakers from Canterbury, N.H. and Sabbathday Lake, Me. LP. Cleveland: Western Reserve University Press, 1961. 250 copies. (The ten records in this series cover data on Shaker history, industries and invention, education and entertainment, religion, the twelve Christian virtues, cookery, covenant, poetry, music, and lives.)

Tortora, Vincent R., composer, *Music of the Shakers.* Cassette. Washington, D.C.: Folkways, The Smithsonian, 1991. (Vincent R. Tortora, director; Glee Clubs of Smith and Amherst Colleges; descriptive folder with song print-outs included; originally recorded as Folkways Record Album FH5378, 1976.)

General Index

Song Index

Song titles enclosed in quotation marks are the titles recorded by the Shaker scribes in their song manuscripts. In the case of songs without manuscript titles, we have assigned the opening words of the songs as titles.